−0. NOV.

# BANNER HEADLINES

# BANNER
# HEADLINES

## STAFFORD SOMERFIELD

*Editor of the*
*NEWS OF THE WORLD*
*1960–1970*

SCAN
BOOKS

ISBN 0 906360 04 8

© Stafford Somerfield 1979

Typeset by Computacomp (UK) Ltd,
Fort William, Scotland.
Printed and bound in Great Britain by
Redwood Burn Limited, Trowbridge
& Esher for Scan Books, Scan House,
4–8 Church Street, Shoreham by Sea,
West Sussex, Great Britain.

# Dedication

*To all those who marry journalists. They have my deepest sympathy.*

# Contents

|   |   | page |
|---|---|---|
| 1 | How It Started | 9 |
| 2 | Great Adventure | 12 |
| 3 | Enter the Carrs | 19 |
| 4 | Wanted — A Million | 25 |
| 5 | Secret Marriage | 33 |
| 6 | All for a Penny | 37 |
| 7 | Crime and Punishment | 44 |
| 8 | Ten Fags for 2d. | 52 |
| 9 | Corset in Cabinet | 57 |
| 10 | Rift with Lloyd George | 68 |
| 11 | Sentence of Death | 79 |
| 12 | Fifty Years an Editor | 84 |
| 13 | Plot at the Coq d'Or | 89 |
| 14 | When it was Fun | 95 |
| 15 | When it was Sad | 102 |
| 16 | In the Hot Seat | 110 |
| 17 | Man at the Top | 119 |
| 18 | Meeting Top People | 124 |
| 19 | Inside Murder | 134 |
| 20 | Christine Keeler | 139 |
| 21 | As I Saw It | 145 |
| 22 | Take-over | 153 |
| 23 | Round by Round | 162 |
| 24 | Our Ally | 168 |
| 25 | Confrontation | 177 |
| 26 | Disenchantment | 183 |
| 27 | Goodbye to All That | 187 |
| 28 | My Way | 195 |
| 29 | Every Day a Sunday | 200 |
|   | Exit | 203 |

# 1 How It Started

In the cold winter of 1968 there was fought an angry, mud-slinging take-over battle for the News of the World, the Sunday newspaper known to every Briton the world over.

Two families, related to each other, the Carrs and the Jacksons, and a cunning solicitor, Lord Riddell, had, after a shaky start in 1891, run the paper successfully for nearly eighty years. They made it the most widely read of any paper, a household name, a gold mine and a force to be reckoned with. Then, with Riddell long dead, the cousins, a Carr and a Jackson of another generation, became locked together in a bitter, money-grabbing take-over scramble. And the traditional Sunday dish I described on television at the height of the storm as 'British as roast beef and Yorkshire pudding', got a new flavour and a new cook.

Carr and Jackson were finished as newspaper owners and a brash, vigorous Australian, Rupert Murdoch, ruled in their place. He came in as Carr's ally and finished as his master.

Derek Jackson, the aging mystery man of the piece, the Professor only a few of us knew, returned to oblivion. Carr, in broken health, disillusioned, looked unhappily at the scene from his Sussex garden.

Murdoch, the conqueror, pressed on, adding another London national newspaper to his tally to become one of the big men of print in Britain, Australia and the United States.

The News of the World story spans more than a hundred years, but I am particularly concerned with the history from 1891, when a brilliant and erratic man, Henry Lascelles Carr, burst out from South Wales where he ran the Western

Mail, and, with a small group of relatives and friends, bought the News of the World, which was then on its knees. The Bell family started it fifty years earlier. They had seen success in their day, but now their time was over.

With him on his great adventure, Lascelles Carr brought his nephew, Emsley Carr, subsequently Editor for fifty years, Charles Jackson, his brother-in-law, a Cardiff barrister with money, and George Riddell, a London solicitor with brains. Riddell fixed the deal for 'peanuts' and took 192 £10-shares instead of a fee. Out of this he made a fortune, and so did the Carrs and the Jacksons.

My heart warms to Lascelles and Emsley Carr. They were journalists, and I was to sit in Emsley's chair for ten years. But the star of the early days was Riddell, cast for the role of villain, but one of the giants of the newspaper game between the wars. In his way he was as big as Northcliffe or Beaverbrook. Round him the early part of the story centres, for this tough, saturnine, scheming solicitor who advised Lascelles Carr, not only became chief proprietor of the News of the World, but was the man behind Lloyd George, the Welsh Wizard and leader of the nation in World War I.

Lascelles Carr, writer and inventor, who didn't give two hoots for anyone, wasn't to last long. He left England mysteriously and died happily in France with a new young wife. Ordered not to drink or smoke, he said life wouldn't be worth living like that and refused to listen; but the doctors were right.

So exit Lascelles. Emsley Carr, his nephew and son-in-law, became Chairman of the company, saw the paper to greatness and died in the job. Years later his youngest son, William, took over, and was in command in 1968 when Murdoch arrived on a plane from Sydney, to fight and win the battle of Bouverie Street.

Charles Jackson was of no great importance except that he had money. He knew nothing about newspapers and was, for a short while, an undistinguished Chairman, for which he was awarded a baronetcy. He wrote a book about silver, still the definitive work on the subject, and sired twin sons. One of them became Professor Jackson, war-hero and scientist. He was the man who put his shares on the market and began the take-over scramble of 1968.

The Professor manoeuvred in Paris and Geneva, for his family's financial benefit, while his cousin, Sir William, gravely ill, fought for the newspaper. The Professor, having taken a sixth wife, was much concerned in his declining years about death duties. There was one answer, he decided, and that was to sell the vast newspaper holding which had come to him and his family through his father.

The fact that the then Socialist MP, Robert Maxwell, nearly won the battle for the News of the World did not concern him, although the Professor's political views were hardly left-wing. Maxwell, a tough, successful publisher, made a bold bid for the paper, and Carr brought in Murdoch to help fight him off. The tussle was vicious, exciting and to the death. Murdoch won. I, as Editor, played some part in the struggle.

# 2 Great Adventure

In 1891 great changes were about to take place in the *News of the World*.

The reason was simple: the proprietors, Walter John Bell and Adolphus William Bell, had been in difficulties since 1888 and, after three more years without improvement, they had to sell. Financial difficulties were not unknown to the Bells, a distinguished family of publishers.

One man who knew about their problems was Thomas Owen of Cardiff, who was associated with that city's morning newspaper, the Western Mail. The Owens were paper-makers and the Bells were their customers.

When the affair of the Bell brothers came to a head, they discussed them with Thomas Owen, who brought in Lascelles Carr, the Western Mail's Editor. Legal advice was necessary, so Mr Carr sent for George Riddell, an energetic young solicitor who acted as London agent for their Cardiff legal advisers, Morgan Scott and Scott.

The News of the World was not then the mighty publication known today throughout the world, with a circulation which once reached eight million, surpassing that of any other English-language newspaper. Then it was produced in tiny premises off London's Strand, and sold rather fewer than fifty thousand copies a week.

But even then the paper had a romantic history. It was already nearly fifty years old, the first copy having appeared on 1 October 1843. The original poster was headed — with commendable foresight — 'News For The Million' and announced, with no false modesty, that it was 'The Novelty of Nations, the wonder of the world', and that the price for forty-eight large, folio columns was only 3d.

'It would contain,' it said 'all the news of the week, printed with a new, distinct and elegant type,' and orders for the 'cheapest, largest and best newspaper' could be placed with all dealers in newspapers, and at the head office, a bow-fronted house of three storeys, and an attic in Holywell Street in the Strand.

Responsible for the new paper was John Browne Bell, son of the man rightly described as the father of the Sunday Press. John Bell lived for eighty-six exciting years between 1745 and 1831, and was, at one time or another, the founder, or proprietor, of nearly a dozen publications.

The one we are concerned with is Bell's Weekly Messenger, founded in 1796, from which sprang Bell's New Weekly Messenger in 1832, which, in turn, was succeeded and absorbed by the News of the World.

John Bell was a master of the craft of book-binding. When he turned to newspapers it was said that 'his taste in putting forth a publication and getting the best artists to adorn it, was new in these times and may be admired in any'. He was known among printers as being the first in the craft to discard the long 's', and was the pioneer of cheap publishing.

Bell's first premises were near Somerset House in the Strand. There was a long garden leading down to the river, and in it stood the printing and book-binding works. Here is a contemporary description of Bell: 'A plain man with a red face and a nose exaggerated by intemperance, and yet there was something not unpleasing in his countenance, especially when he spoke.' It was also said of him that he had 'black, sparkling eyes, a good-natured smile, and gentlemanly manners'.

He was Bookseller to the Prince of Wales. Another who helped him was Captain Edward Topham, an adjutant in the Horse Guards, and one of the town's most fashionable men: 'He maintained a gorgeous phaeton and wrote broad farces and epilogues.' Apparently the Prince, Bell and Topham had much in common, for Leigh Hunt, the historian wrote: 'Unfortunately for Bell he had as great a taste for wines and neat ankles as for pretty books.' The same remark would apply to other members of the trio.

Bell and Topham had a disagreement in 1789 and separated. Bell went merrily on his way until 1793 when, unhappily for him, he libelled the Foot Guards. The Times 6 February 1783 reports that he was called up to appear for judgement and, not appearing, process of the Court was issued against him. His principal and most famous publication was sold.

But the bold John Bell was by no means finished. He went out to Flanders as a war correspondent, and was sufficiently important to be described by a jealous contemporary as 'a bloody satellite of Robespierre and a promoter of Jacobite heresies'. By 1795 he was in trouble once more and, after much litigation, he became bankrupt, but this again was but a challenge.

In March 1796 he issued his Weekly Messenger, and the prospectus was backed with, among others, the names of the Prince of Wales, the Duke of York, the Duke of Clarence and the Lord Mayor of London. The objects of the paper were 'to be useful to merchants, men of fashion, ladies of quality and, above all, to the community in general'.

Thus was born the enterprise on which R. Power Berrey, much later assistant Editor of the News of the World, commented: 'The Messenger owed its success to Bell's fiery energy, original ideas, nose for news, typographical skill, vivid writing and genius for advertising ... The Sunday Press still shows traces of his influence, and there is little doubt that the first Gordon Bennett, the Scotsman who, with his New York Herald, originated modern American journalism in 1835, copied Bell's methods.'

His paper prospered. By 1803 it had a circulation of six thousand copies and the Nelson Funeral number topped fourteen thousand. By 1812 an official return showed that the Weekly Messenger was second in order of circulation and, some years before his death — at Fulham in 1831 —

John Bell had made a fortune.

So passed the father of Sunday newspapers, who left not only a great tradition, but a son as adventurous and courageous as himself — John Browne Bell. This Bell began as a publisher in rivalry to his father, and there was much ill-feeling between them. Apparently Bell Senior did not approve of the sturdy independence of his son. The son lost the first battle. In 1812 he took the path to the bankruptcy court, as his father had done, but, like his father, he was by no means 'down and out'. Assisted by his imaginative and energetic wife, Mary Ann, he was soon heard of again. Mrs Bell was an acknowledged leader of the fashions of the period, and this announcement in the World of Fashion gives some indication of her activity.

This publication is indebted to Mrs Bell, removed to No. 3 Cleveland Row, opposite St James's Palace, for the designs and the selections of the 'Fashions and the Costumes of All Nations' which regularly embellish it. Mrs Bell's Magazin de Modes is replete with every fashionable article: and at which there is a daily and constant succession of Novelties in Millinery, Dresses, etc., etc., and at Most Moderate Prices. Mrs Bell's Patent Corsets are unrivalled, and very superior to all others; they impart an indescribable grace and elegance to the figure.

On 1 January 1832, John Browne Bell took another leaf from his father's book. He produced the first issue of his Sunday paper, the New Weekly Messenger, which he issued from 2 Surrey Street, Strand. It was almost a replica of John Bell Senior's publication and the first front page contained long extracts from other newspapers.

Ten years later he was planning the News of the World and the first copy appeared on 1 October 1843. The leader, written by John Browne Bell himself, presented to the public the new paper. Modestly it 'abstains from elaborate introductory observations', but hopes that public opinion will pronounce it 'the Best as well as the Largest and Cheapest, of all the newspapers published'.

It pledged that 'upon no account shall any alteration ever be made in the price. We intend, and are resolved, that it shall be sold for Threepence only'. Alas, that promise, like others, wasn't kept. John Browne Bell could not foresee the astronomical publishing costs of modern times.

And so the paper was launched and almost immediately the proprietor ran into trouble. The difficulty was the price — 5½d. less than others. The people welcomed the paper but the newsvendors hated this first experiment in cheap newspapers. They believed it meant lost profits to them.

They met at the Crown and Anchor in the Strand and a deputation waited on Bell. But they had underestimated his character. Sending them about their business, he spoke words as true now as they were in 1843: 'The public will buy my paper, gentlemen.' His written reply has an even more topical ring: 'The proprietors do not admit the right of any individual to dictate to them at what price they shall, or shall not, offer a newspaper to the British public. They consider such dictation an unwarrantable interference with the spirit of commercial enterprise (by which this country has been raised to its present greatness and upon which it mainly depends), as well as a monstrous interference to prevent the public from enjoying the advantage of a cheap and interesting political and family newspaper.'

Bell declared on his front page: 'To give the poorer classes of society a paper that would suit their means, and to the middle as well as to the richer, a journal which from its immense circulation should command their attention, have been the influencing motives which have caused the appearance of the News of the World ... we shall not be wanting in our duty. We have neither prejudices to forego nor passion to conciliate. Our motto is *Truth*. Our practice is the *fearless advocacy of truth*.'

It would be good journalism even today, when there is

great need for such sturdy independence and courage.

John Browne Bell won his fight. He posted circulars to the provincial agents, offering to send them supplies of the paper direct from the office. They seized the opportunity and, from that day, it became obtainable in every town and village in the country. Meanwhile, his fighting spirit aroused, the Editor flayed the newsvendors for their 'shameful conspiracy', and their attempt to 'suppress cheap knowledge'. He was winning all the way.

The paper grew. In 1852 it moved to new premises in Exeter Street in the Strand, London, and in 1854 the circulation soared as people bought it to read the latest news from the war front — the Crimea. There were vivid accounts of the Charge of the Light Brigade, the Battle of Inkerman, the Assault on the Redan and the Surrender of Sebastopol. Soon it was to announce that Britain was at peace again.

And in 1855 peace came also to John Browne Bell. He died at Campden Hill, Kensington, aged seventy-seven, surrounded by his family. He had led a turbulent, bold and satisfying life, which began with upheaval, went on to meet and conquer disaster, and finally triumphed. Before he died he received news that his paper — and it was truly his paper — had a greater sale than any other weekly newspaper.

His will split the property into shares and appointed the eldest son, John William, trustee. A solicitor, it was soon apparent that he had not inherited the fighting qualities of his father and his grandfather. With the stamp duty on newspapers abolished, now was the moment to reduce the price. He should have led the field. His was the pioneer of cheap newspapers; it was the ideal for which Bell's ancestors had gone into action. But John William Bell faltered. He applied to the Court of Chancery for advice and was told it was for him to make the decision. Still he hesitated and, while he was doing so, the other Sunday newspapers forestalled him. They came down in price. He reaped the reward of one who hesitates. When he died in

1877, after twenty-two years of trusteeship, he left behind the wreck of a great newspaper.

After John William Bell, in came his sons, Walter John and Adolphus William Bell, who waited nearly three years before reducing the price of the paper to 1d. on 2 May 1880. The move acted as a blood transfusion. The circulation turned the corner and began to forge ahead. But, at this moment, the brothers were forced to fight a legal action brought by their cousin, a daughter of Horace Bell, one of the founder's sons. Tired of receiving no dividends since the fall in the paper's popularity, she thought the way to get some money was by selling the property.

The Master of the Rolls ordered a valuation, and the brothers Bell were permitted by the Court to buy out the remaining proprietors for about £4,000. They became the sole owners. From this position they pushed the circulation up to 80,000. But they were too late. Rivals had not only reduced their prices to 1d. but had increased their sizes. The News of the World was slow on both counts. The moment called for the imagination and courage of the founder, but the grandsons had neither his touch nor his character.

The brothers stood still. Slowly the circulation dwindled and by 1890 it was down to under 50,000. The situation was critical and it was at that moment that the Bells told Thomas Owen about their plight and the meeting with Lascelles Carr was arranged.

It was the beginning of a new era.

# 3  Enter the Carrs

Henry Lascelles Carr, the man behind the reorganisation of the paper in 1891, was an experienced journalist and manager. His skill was gained doing the job and fighting against odds. He had immense moral courage, imagination and drive. Lloyd George said of him: 'He is the cleverest man I ever met.'

The son of James Carr, a Wesleyan Minister of Knottingley, near Pontefract in Yorkshire, and Martha Carr (*née* Hay), Lascelles Carr was born at 9·30 in the morning of 26 May 1841. His early life was spent in the north and it was intended that he should follow his father into the ministry. But while a student he wrote an article for the Liverpool Daily Post, and the Editor persuaded him that his future lay in newspapers rather than the church. Having smelled printers' ink, Lascelles agreed. He became a sub-editor on the Post, and, while there, wrote an article on economics which was read by the Marquess of Bute, who was about to start a paper in Cardiff. He wrote to Carr and asked him to come to see him.

Carr was twenty-eight, and the year 1869. The opportunity given him would excite any young newspaper man. Everything was against the paper, said Bute: politically it would support the Conservatives in a land of Liberals; it would champion the causes of the coal-owners and the Church in a radical hot-bed. Fainter hearts would have caught the next train home, but not Lascelles Carr. He stayed and was appointed assistant-editor.

The paper was the Western Mail. Started on a shoe-string, its original home was in an old salt store, a dilapidated building always threatening to fall down, and the first printing-machines were bought second-hand from the Western Morning News of Plymouth. The engineer, who brought the machines to Cardiff, had £5 towards his expenses and a hammer and spanner in his pockets. He set off for Plymouth and spent the first night at Bristol, paying 1s. 6d. for bed and breakfast. Single-handed, he dismantled the machines, and a number of unemployed old soldiers and sailors did the hoisting and lifting. By road, rail and water he got the machines back to Cardiff.

They were installed in the salt store and made ready to be driven by an old vertical engine brought up from the docks. The pages were prepared, and the editor stood waiting for the first copy, a hunk of bread and cheese in his hand. He'd had nothing to eat all day.

Tapes flew off, sheets of paper lost their way and went wandering into the bowels of the press. A man was sent in head-first to sort out the tangle, and, to add to the gaiety, the worker selected had an impediment in his speech. From somewhere underneath the machinery could be heard his stammered curses. But the first Western Mail appeared, even though the type became loose and the spaces came up and pock-marked all the impressions. Worse still, many of the spaces printed the name of the type-founders, and the people of Cardiff were left wondering why the name Figgins, Figgins, Figgins, appeared all over their new paper. But the child was born.

In 1877 Lord Bute decided to sell the paper, and Lascelles Carr, Daniel Owen and others raised enough money to buy it. Carr became Editor.

In its early days the Western Mail was thoroughly hated by the Radicals, who predicted its early end. But, as the years passed, a change in public opinion took place. The people of Cardiff slowly began to realise that, in Lascelles Carr, they had a champion, a man who hated injustice and who would support a good cause, regardless of politics.

The boldest line he ever took was to maintain the right of workmen 'to combine for the purpose of improving their position, and to choose such leaders as they may think best qualified to guide their counsels and conduct their affairs'. This statement was written by Carr over a hundred years ago and, what is more, in a Conservative newspaper. He hit out at 'scandalous conditions in the mining valleys'; he condemned fever factories, and declared that the colliers should be treated as reasonable men, and not as machines. An indignant Conservative declared: 'The biggest Radical in Wales is Lascelles Carr'. Lascelles saw no reason why Conservatives should not stand for fair play and better conditions for the workers.

Often impatient, he did not suffer fools gladly. Woe betide anyone guilty of careless work. By nature he was a Bohemian, and Emsley Carr, his nephew, wrote:

Coming as a schoolboy of eighteen from the north to begin my journalistic career I was amazed at the free-and-easy life which the members of the staff apparently led. In the early 'eighties on an occasional holiday I had seen something of this provincial Bohemia, and wondered how it was possible for the paper to be produced. Directly I became part of the organisation I discovered that all this was on the surface. The stolid decorum of a bank or the dull routine of a city office might not characterise it, but discipline there was and that of a rigid character. A 'miss' was a crime, a slovenly written article past forgiveness.

The paper advocated town bands, public parks and military displays. The Editor did not believe that dull, lifeless Sundays made people happier or better. The Chapel folk were shocked. To rant against drunkenness was not enough, said Carr. Something had to be done to entertain those who spent most of their lives doing hard, dirty, back-aching work. He resolutely opposed the Sunday Closing Act, describing it as a 'national disgrace and absolute tyranny'. The licensed victuallers of England and Wales wanted to give Carr a testimonial, but he would accept nothing that would impede his liberty of action and asked instead that subscriptions should be sent to the infirmary.

When the paper celebrated its jubilee in 1919, the President of the Welsh Miners' Federation wrote: 'The paper's valuable and continuous work on behalf of Wales and Welsh national movements is part of the secret, I think, of the success and prosperity of this Tory organ among a people the great majority of whom detest most heartily its politics.'

Lascelles Carr was an inventor as well as an editor. He made one of the first bicycles with his own hands, and the strange machine was the wonder of Cardiff. It collapsed and nearly ended his career. He had a theory that all rifles were designed on the wrong principle, since the straight stock ignored the fact that the human arm is crooked and out of angle with the eye. So he made a gun of his own with a jointed stock and used it without disaster. He also invented an incubator but, when the first chick was born, he was so excited that he left the door open. The rest of the eggs went cold and he finished off the incubator with one blow.

He had a sense of humour. Awakened one night by burglars, he fired a gun out of the window to attract the local policeman who, he said, was paid 30s. a week for tackling precisely that kind of situation. When a hard-up solicitor called at his office, Lascelles required him to write in the visitors' book that, in consideration of a gift of money, he solemnly undertook to relieve the premises for a period of one year of the 'nuisance of his obnoxious person'.

Carr called the editorial staff to his house to witness his power over bees. He explained that, to a man who knew his business, bees were as harmless as butterflies. Then he stepped forward to the apiary. The next moment he was in full flight. Then he took to sailing in a coracle on the river Taff, and nearly drowned himself.

When a fire destroyed the Western Mail offices on 3 June

1893, Lascelles was at his best. While the building was in flames and it was evident that the plant and machinery would be wrecked, his mind was active with one problem: How would the paper be brought out?

It was a Saturday night. He had only Sunday to get the job done if there was to be a paper on Monday morning. While others fought the flames, he made arrangements with a firm at Newport, a nearby town, to lend him a press. But there was no power to drive it. That didn't stop him. He acquired a traction steam-engine — one of those with a big flywheel and a tall chimney, often seen in the old days in farmyards driving threshing machines — and had it placed up against the building. His next order was that a hole should be made in the wall and belting passed through. Within a short time the engine was coupled to the press and, with his heart in his mouth, he gave the order for it to be started up. It worked.

Next came the job of producing the paper, which Carr and his shirt-sleeved staff raced to do on time, making the splash the story of their own fire.

This was the man who, with friends, took over the News of the World in 1891, and appointed his young nephew, Emsley, to edit it. It was typical of Lascelles that, when placed on a strict diet, he wrote to a colleague: 'I was so miserable when I was told to give up drinking and smoking that I decided that to continue to live on these terms was not worthwhile.'

His health suffered and, after his wife died in 1900, he was persuaded to live in a warmer climate. He went to France, married again and died in 1902 at Hyeres, aged sixty-one.

David Davies, Editor of the South Wales Daily Post wrote this description of him:

A round, squat little figure, my first impression was that he wore particularly ugly boots. He had views regarding the manner in which feet should be shod and had designed his own boots. His demeanour was scarcely less disturbing. The full face, with beetling brow, surmounted by a thick tangle of hair, the spectacled eyes that seemed to glare through the glasses, the deep chesty voice jerking out asthmatic sentences, conspired to freeze the timid. But he had nevertheless a winning way, if abrupt and impulsive — the rough exterior covered one of the most tender of hearts.

# 4 Wanted — A Million

By 12 May 1891 financial arrangements for the sale of the News of the World were completed, and the vendors, the brothers Bell, assigned the remainder of the lease of 19 Exeter Street, for which the new company agreed to pay £85 a year. The total share value of the new company was £20,000, divided into two thousand shares of £10 each. Of these the Bells took 1,500, and 497 were allocated to Lascelles Carr and his colleague from Wales, J. G. Gunn. Three others had one share each. The new plans quickly went ahead. On 18 May the directors met at 19 Exeter Street, and G. A. Riddell, solicitor, was appointed secretary. Since there was no money to pay him, he took 192 shares from the other directors in lieu of fees. More than anyone else he came to be responsible for the financial success of the paper.

George Allardice Riddell was born on 25 May 1865 at 2 Stanhope Place, Loughborough Road, Brixton, London, a small semi-detached house in the maze of lower-middle-class streets on the south side of the Thames. No round plaque marks the birthplace of the man who became a friend of statesmen, a peer of the·realm, chairman of the world's largest circulation newspaper, and twice a millionaire.

George Riddell's father was James Riddell, a photographer. The Riddell family originally came from Duns in Berwickshire, and it was believed that Riddell was born in Scotland. This was not so, though reference books and on his death, The Times, stated that he was born in Duns, son of a civil servant. Riddell himself had encouraged the belief that he came from Scotland, but in fact (as he was the first to discover) his grandfather, George Riddell, after whom he was named, left there in the 1800s to seek his fortune in Peru, taking his wife and family with him. There he died, leaving two children, James, who was Riddell's father, and a daughter, adopted while a schoolgirl by a minister. At the age of twenty she married an English merchant of Valparaiso, David William Allardice, who had business connections with Liverpool and a house at Rock Ferry, Cheshire. He was to play an important part in Riddell's early life.

James returned to England at the age of twenty-four. He had many jobs but did not remain long in any of them, and when, in 1864, he first got to know Isabel Young, he was trying his hand at photography — then a comparatively new invention. Isabel's family had come from Scotland and her father was a piano-maker in Lambeth, living at 13 Richmond Terrace, Thorne Road. They were devout Presbyterians. It was not long before James moved into Richmond Terrace, as a lodger. He married Isabel at Clapham Presbyterian Church, where the young couple had first met, on 19 July 1864. Both were twenty-five and they went to live at Stanhope Place in Brixton, where, ten months later, their son George was born. James had weak lungs and he died on 3 April 1867, with his son not yet three.

Isabel went back to her parents, taking her baby with her. There was certainly no need for Riddell to have been ashamed of his upbringing, but he was, and kept it secret. (Unravelling the truth was a fascinating exercise.) His mother taught him to read, especially from the Bible, lessons he never forgot, and sent him to a South London church school. Her sister-in-law, married to D. W. Allardice, encouraged her husband to help the young Mrs Riddell, and he made her a small allowance from which she provided clothes for herself and young George.

Visits to his uncle played an important part in George's life. Mr and Mrs Allardice were impressed by the boy, who was bright and alert. They had a daughter, Annie, with whom George was allowed to go for walks. The cousins got to know each other very well and, many years later, she became Riddell's second wife. The Riddells were very much 'the poor relations' and George, while only a boy, was conscious of it. 'One day,' he said to his cousin, 'I'll be a millionaire, and I'll show them.'

Mr Allardice promised his sister-in-law to start the boy off in the London office of his solicitor, O. B. Wooler of Darlington. If George showed promise, Allardice undertook to provide for his articles.

So young Riddell started work as an office-boy with Octavius Borrodaile Wooler, at 9 John Street, Bedford Row, London. In October of that year, 1882, at the age of eighteen, he passed the preliminary examination of the Law Society and was articled on 20 August 1883. At the end of five years he took his final, passed with First Class Honours and won the Law Society's prize.

A description of the office in which he worked, first as office-boy and then as pupil, is given by Riddell in a book he wrote for private circulation fifty years later.

The clerk was a musty-looking, middle-aged man with a clipped beard, shaved upper lip, and shabby frock coat. His room was large and lofty with two spacious windows. The oak floor, none too clean, had no carpet but a mat was provided at the clerk's feet. A table and seven chairs comprised the only furniture in the room, unless a number of black tin boxes could be counted as furniture. The table was covered with bundles of papers, some large, some small, but all tied up neatly with red tape. The room had not been changed for fifty years.

Riddell and his mother moved to Stroud Green Road, Finsbury Park, North London. Both house and contents were given to her by her parents on their death. From there George Riddell went to work each day, travelling by horse-

27

bus and foot to Mr Wooler's office.

Riddell described himself as 'a penniless articled clerk', with a consuming ambition to save £20,000 and retire at seventy. Though he was to achieve the first part of his ambition many times over, he failed to achieve the second by a matter of months.

His early struggles taught him to eat little and walk to save bus fares. Once he stood on King's Cross Station with the price of a bun or a newspaper in his pocket. What was he to do? Eat or buy a paper and search the advertisement columns for a job? He chose the newspaper and went hungry.

Riddell has described how he made his first sovereign. He was told to take a letter round to a gentleman's house and wait for the answer. By walking quickly he was able to save the fare which he felt entitled to claim. Arriving at the house, he was shown into the library and asked to wait. While doing so he glanced at the books. The door opened and the owner entered the library.

'I see you are interested in the books,' he said. 'They are first editions and extremely valuable. One is missing. If you ever come across it, come along to me and I will give you the price of the book and a sovereign for your trouble.'

Young Riddell hurried out and for weeks spent all his spare time in the second-hand bookshops of Charing Cross Road. One day, to his delight, he found the missing volume. He rushed away to collect the reward. A cousin told a different version. She said Riddel saw a book collector's advertisement and remembered that a volume required was in his grandfather's house in Clapham. He took it without permission and sold it.

In the year he became a solicitor Riddell was a tall, slim figure. He appeared much older than his years and was invariably dressed in black, a tall Gladstone collar encircling his long thin neck. He wore mutton-chop whiskers and had a clean-shaven chin. He walked with long strides, and on his head was perched a hard, tall hat, something between a topper and a bowler. Sometimes he was taken for a Methodist preacher, especially when he quoted the Scriptures, which he had a habit of doing. He worked twelve hours a day and studied late into the night.

Near his mother's house in Hornsey Rise Gardens lived Grace Edith Williams, a young woman of about his own age, whom he had noticed out walking with her sister. He learned that the family had come from Wales. Grace was pretty, her hair dark, her figure neat and her voice musical. George was invited to meet the Williams family and Grace went to see Mrs Riddell. George became fond of her; moreover, she had a little money.

Now that he was qualified, he was in charge of Mr Wooler's London office and he planned to take over the practice. He discussed the proposition with Grace's family. They were prepared to put up £300, and although that was not enough, there were other young solicitors about with a little capital who were ready to come in with him. Soon the name of O. B. Wooler disappeared from 9 John Street, Bedford Row, and in its place appeared three new names: Riddel, Vaizey and Smith. At the age of twenty-three, George Riddell was the senior partner.

As so often with Riddell's affairs there is a mystery about the way it was done. He said he came into the office to learn, to his horror, that old Wooler had suddenly died. He had to take over. But official records show that Mr Wooler died in retirement at Darlington, many years later.

In the same year as he qualified and founded Riddell, Vaizey and Smith, Riddell married Grace Williams. Riddell's mother let her son take over her house and keep the best pieces of furniture. And so, on their wedding day, George and Grace moved in and the widowed mother went off to a room in Kilburn.

The marriage took place at St Mary's, Hornsey Rise, in the parish of Islington, on 13 December 1888. The bridegroom described himself as a bachelor, solicitor by profession, residing at 9 John Street, Bedford Row, the address of his office. Grace Edith Williams, aged twenty-four, was described as a spinster of No 57 Hornsey Rise Gardens. Both witnesses were members of the Williams family. No members of the Riddell family were present.

On his wedding morning George went to work as usual. At eleven o'clock he took an hour off for the ceremony and afterwards returned to work. There was no honeymoon. Riddell said he couldn't afford one. He was at his desk every morning before nine o'clock, seldom stopped for lunch, and would still be working when the clerks went home. Interviews would take up most of the day and, at six, he would start dictating his letters, which had to be written by hand, and a pressing taken for the copy before the rush, by the clerks, to catch the nine-thirty post. Saturdays and Sundays were the same as any other working-day.

He drove his staff relentlessly. Clerks would tremble when he shouted for them. Some bolstered up their courage with a quick drink at the pub next door, but this was a sure way to incur his displeasure. It was monstrous, he said, that they should waste on beer the money he paid them. Later, he bought the pub, saying he might as well get his money back.

One clerk, liking his drink, invariably took a clove to disguise the smell. Riddell suffered for years in silence, but one day there were no cloves available, and the clerk ate an onion instead. As bad luck would have it Riddell sent for him. 'For years I've had to stand the smell of beer and cloves.' he exploded. 'But I'm damned if I'll put up with beer and pickled onions.'

Riddell's great interest was property. Throughout his life he believed in bricks and mortar. 'Take a quick profit,' was his advice, adding: 'A man never became bankrupt by taking a profit.' On Saturday and Sunday afternoons he would hire a hansom and drive round the streets of London, leaving no area untouched. He never gave the cabby a tip. 'No-one ever tips me,' he said.

When a rich man, he would use a hansom to go to his office but would never pay through the trap-door in the roof. When the cab stopped he would climb down and place the exact fare on the top of the wheel, so that the driver had to come down from his perch to get his money. Meanwhile, Riddell would be climbing the stone steps to the front door, his ears pricked for the cabby's curses. When they came, Riddell would turn, fix his cold, blue eyes on the driver, and treat him and the whole street to a stream of invective. One cabby, smarting under the outburst, threatened Riddell with the law. 'You bloody fool,' was the response. 'What do you know of the law? You can't distinguish between slander and mere vulgar abuse.'

In his first year as a solicitor, not yet twenty-five he made £10,000. He particularly liked corner sites, for they provided the greatest chance for development. 'If the development isn't on one side, it will be on the other.' he said. Sometimes stubborn occupiers had to be removed from properties he had marked down. He was ruthless. In those days tenants had few rights under the law, and he harried them to the limit. His dictum was: 'When conciliation fails, crush.'

'I can't afford mercy,' he used to say. And if he were thwarted, the man or woman who had stood in his way would be carefully noted, no matter how trivial the incident. He was always willing to take a calculated risk, though not on something in which he played no part. He would gamble if he could influence the result by his own skill, energy and ruthlessness, but not if it was something outside his control. This was his view on speculating on the Stock Exchange: 'It's like jumping a chasm — with each success comes the urge to jump a bigger one; finally the jumper comes to a chasm too big for him, falls and breaks his neck.'

In forty years his clerk never got home before ten. Once he asked if he might go to evening classes. 'Certainly,' said Riddell, 'you should try to improve yourself. What time do you want to go? Seven o'clock? Well, you're always finished by then.' The clerk went to classes once, so he told me when an old man.

Riddell usually dined at the First Avenue Hotel in Holborn, his meal consisting of a chop, a piece of bread and a glass of water — his digestion was poor. He permitted himself one luxury — a sixpenny cigar — although he never bought a box. 'He was terrified someone might steal one,' said his clerk.

The clerk, once faced with imprisonment for debt, took his courage in his hands to tell his hard-luck story just as Riddell finished dictating hundreds of words. His notebook was full. 'It's a good job you've told me now,' growled Riddell. 'You can bloody well write out these notes while you're inside.' But the clerk was too valuable to be allowed to go to prison. Riddell paid his debts and deducted the amount by instalments from his pay.

Riddell's problem, at this time, was to raise enough capital to buy property. In those days bank managers had far more discretion about overdrafts than today, and when he went to his bank, the manager knew what he was after. Riddell would cajole, threaten if necessary, to get the cash he wanted. Meeting a colleague, the worried manager almost wept: 'He comes down with nice words, and if that fails he shouts and threatens to take away his account. I always have to give him what he wants.'

It was so throughout his life; Riddell rarely failed to get what he wanted.

# 5 Secret Marriage

Just as Riddell never revealed the place of his birth, so in later years he kept complete silence about his first wife, Grace. No mention was made of her in reference books. 'My first wife was a drunkard,' he once said, 'and life with her became impossible.'*

One thing is certain, he neglected Grace. Callers at their house would be told that Mrs Riddell was not in good health; that she had a headache; that she had gone to lie down. Riddell himself told a cousin, whom I met: 'One evening I arrived home from the office and asked the maid where Mrs Riddell was. The reply made me furiously angry. I could have struck the servant. "She's lying down, but it's time you knew what the trouble is. She's drunk!" ' Riddell rushed upstairs and a furious row followed. He decided they must leave Finsbury Park immediately.

The couple moved to Museum Street, where they took a flat near Riddell's office. Grace promised to reform. Perhaps, as they were near the office, George would be able to give her more of his time. But he found every day completely full. Always now, a shorthand writer was sent round to his rooms at seven in the morning and Riddell dictated as he shaved. Then started the long day at the office, a quick dinner, usually at a restaurant, more work and home again near midnight.

One day, according to Riddell, Grace was brought home by the police. She had been found drunk in the street. This was the last straw, he said; he walked out and left her.

* It took me months to track the papers and documents, but the story, never before revealed, became increasingly fascinating as I uncovered one secret after another.

Riddell became the London agent of Morgan, Scott and Scott, the Cardiff solicitors, and made many trips to Wales. It was there that he made the contacts which put him in the big money. He didn't waste time on the train journey, nor on the way to the station. A clerk always accompanied him and took notes while riding in the cab. Often the 'Yours faithfully' was added while Riddell leaned from the carriage window as the train pulled out.

At this time he travelled third-class, but he resented the intrusion of others in the compartment, especially as he had generally covered both seats with his papers. The black-coated figure worked without pause until the train drew into Cardiff. Later he treated himself to a first-class ticket, which he regarded as a saving: there were fewer interruptions, so he could work harder and make-up for the increased cost.

Cardiff was booming in the 'nineties. There were great developments in both rail and tramway transport. Riddell's new acquaintances in Wales were alert to the possibilities and they prospered. Income tax was no problem, varying as it did between 6d. and 8d. in the pound: it later fell to 2d.

The number of callers at Riddell's office in Bedford Row grew, and the staff was enlarged to include sixteen clerks, and the house next door and the printing works behind, were purchased.

One caller at 9 John Street was different. She came regularly every month, a little old-fashioned body, dressed in black and wearing a bonnet. Dignified and proud, she would quietly ask for Mr Riddell. Generally he was too busy to see her, but the clerk would bring his message, a golden sovereign. With a sad smile she would take it and, modestly turning her back, would pull up her flowing black skirt and place the sovereign in a pocket at her waist. Before turning to say 'Good afternoon' to the clerk, the outside skirt would be smoothed down and the bonnet re-adjusted. Then she would walk out without another word. In his own way Riddell was keeping his promise to provide for his mother.

Grace made embarrassing visits to the office. She begged forgiveness, but Riddell's mind was made up. Grace would receive an allowance and, if she did not stop coming to him, he would take steps to see that she was prevented from doing so. They had been married less than five years.

Grace consulted solicitors, and on 8 August 1893 in the High Court Mr Justice Barnes ordered that 'George Allardice Riddell do within fourteen days from the service of this order on him return home to the petitioner and render to her conjugal rights'. Riddell did not appear or defend the suit, nor did he return as ordered in fourteen days. He didn't return at all.

Grace received from him an allowance of £300 a year, and it was never varied. Sometimes she would write to him, and there were still times when she called at his office, asking for help. On these occasions, a secretary would be despatched with a sovereign and instructions to tell Grace of the folly of living beyond her income, and to issue a strict warning that no more money would be forthcoming.

By 1900, after seven years, in which he had worked hard and prospered and 'had not denied himself the pleasure of female company', as one who knew him delicately put it, Riddell wished to marry again. So did Grace. On 2 April 1900 their marriage was dissolved 'by reason that since the marriage celebration the said respondent had been guilty of adultery and non-compliance with a decree for restitution of conjugal rights dated 8 August 1893'. Riddell did not appear and was ordered to pay costs. Six months later, on 29 October 1900, the President of the Divorce Court granted the decree absolute. After twelve years the couple had regained their freedom.

Riddell's staff learned about the case by accident. A clerk, visiting the law courts, saw the names in the list. Just at that moment Riddell himself appeared and ordered the clerk back to the office. He was very angry. He had gone to a Holborn firm of solicitors in the utmost secrecy to arrange matters, and that morning on leaving for the court had announced that he was going to see a client. Divorce was a dirty word in those days.

That evening Riddell called at St Thomas's Hospital on Miss Allardice, daughter of the uncle who had befriended him and his mother. The man who had given him his start. Annie, aged thirty-five and of independent means, had entered the Nightingale School at St Thomas's as a probationer and, after little more than a year's training, had joined the hospital staff as a nurse, later to become a ward sister. So once again she met her cousin George, now a rising solicitor.

Their marriage took place on 2 November 1900, at All Souls, Marylebone. The certificate described him as 'single and unmarried'. He too was thirty-five. James Riddell, his father, was noted as 'a gentleman ... deceased'. At the birth of his son, James had been content to register himself as a photographer.

Riddell behaved on the morning of his second marriage exactly as on the first. He went to work. A partner met him on the stairs. 'I can't stop now,' said Riddell. 'I've got an important engagement. As a matter of fact I'm going to be married.' He shouted to the office boy: 'Go round to the rank in Bedford Row and get me a cab. Better make it one with a white horse.' Apart from the witnesses — Annie's brother and Riddell's pupil — the vicar, the bride and bridegroom, no one attended the ceremony. No newspaper report was printed.

Grace waited less than four months after the decree absolute before she married Henry Christopher Manners, a customs officer, on 12 February 1901, at Christ Church, High Harrogate. Manners retired from the customs service and went to live with Grace at 109 Redlands Road, Bristol, where he eventually died on 13 March 1913, leaving £1,636. 11s. 7d. Grace then went to live at 135 Crouch Hill, Crouch End, Middlesex. She died on 27 January 1929, aged sixty-five, leaving £35. Her first husband was then a millionaire.

# 6 All for a Penny

What sort of paper was the News of the World when Riddell became secretary of the company? More money was needed. One of the first things required was a new press. The existing machines were too slow and old-fashioned, while the Exeter Street premises off the Strand were inconvenient. The paper had to be enlarged to meet strong competition.

Glancing through old files one notices a passion for detailed and accurate reporting. Executions of the week were a regular feature and the reporter would discuss, without embarrassment, the weight of the victim, the length of the drop and the last words on the scaffold. There was also plenty of scope for comment, such as: 'You made a nice mess of that one,' being the reporter's remark to the hangman, and the faithfully recorded reply: 'They wouldn't take my advice; I would have given him four feet six.'

Revealing also is this account of newspaper enterprise, which told readers exactly how the news was sent in.

When a reporter desires to use the pigeons, he leaves word the night before to the person in charge of them. This is very necessary. When they are to fly far, or on any particular business, it is better that they should only be lightly fed in the morning. The pigeons, two or four, as may be required, are caught in the morning and placed in a comfortable wicker or tin basket — like a small luncheon basket with compartments. The reporter, when he leaves the office, carries the basket with him.

He writes his report very legibly and compactly so as to

put as much on a page of 'flimsy' as it will possibly hold. Then he rolls the 'flimsy' neatly up and attaches it to the leg of the bird by means of an elastic band. The pigeon being released makes straight for home. Arriving at the newspaper office, it alights on the edge of the dovecot. To go through the usual circular-headed opening it pushes before it a couple of light wires and these, falling after it, close the aperture. However the bird is not yet into the cot. It has only gone the length of the trap. This trap, two feet square or so, has a flooring fixed upon an electric spring. The weight of the bird pressing down the spring releases the electric current, which rings a bell in the sub-editor's room. The bird thus heralds its own arrival.

In charge of the business side, Riddell set about the task of building the paper with all the energy he possessed. A date was fixed for delivery of the new press. As the time drew near it became apparent that the makers could not complete their side of the bargain. Riddell attacked. There was talk of a writ and of compensation. Hurried negotiations followed and Riddell was able to arrange terms much more to his liking. The makers were so struck by the young man's tenacity that they invited him to become their solicitor.

Negotiations were started for the lease of 9 and 10 Whitefriars Street, off Fleet Street, in the heart of the newspaper world, and these premises were secured in March 1892. The move was completed two months later, while 19 Exeter Street was leased on good terms to George Newnes Ltd, the publishers of Tit-Bits, and, to complete the deal, the old press was sold for £900 worth of printers' ink.

Now an appeal to the public. In May 1892, with the new machine in Whitefriars Street, the size of the paper was increased to twelve pages, and, on every vacant hoarding in the land, appeared in flaming letters: GOOD OLD NEWS OF THE WORLD. THE LARGEST SUNDAY NEWSPAPER. The battle for circulation was on.

There could be no looking back and, as funds became short, the nominal capital of the company was increased to £30,000 by the creation of one thousand 6 per cent preference shares of £10 each. The issue of 29 May 1892 contained the announcement that 'on and after today the business of the News of the World will be transacted at our new premises, 9 and 10 Whitefriars Street, Fleet Street, EC4, to which address all communications must be forwarded'. There was also a story headed: 'The Machine of the Century. How the News of the World is today produced. A lifelike Press which Prints, Pastes, Folds, Counts and Delivers 25,000 Copies per hour.'

In layout the paper was little changed, but a commentator at the time said the proprietors had modernised it 'not without loss of sedateness'; to modern eyes it seems as sedate as Mrs Grundy.

Sometimes there was not sufficient cash available to pay the wages, and the directors had to put their hands into their own pockets. Often it was necessary to wait for the pennies from sales before bills could be met. Personal guarantees of the directors were required against overdrafts, and frequently those to whom money was owed took shares in the company instead of cash. Those who did so eventually had cause to thank their good luck. One such example was the Phillips family of South Wales. They sold the paper a boiler, needed to drive the machinery, for £200, and in settlement they took 512 shares. By 1950 the market value of those shares had reached £73,000. The paper's racing correspondent could not pay his bookmaker, but persuaded him, reluctantly, to take shares instead. Later they would have paid the original debt a thousand times.

Bob Berry, an assistant editor, used to say that Emsley Carr and himself were at first the only two permanent members of the editorial staff, and that £6 was placed on one side each week to pay their wages. Carr took £3. 10s. and Berry £2. 10s. Sometimes the £6 was not available. Often it was touch and go whether the raw materials of newspaper-making — newsprint and ink — would be forthcoming, and Mr Fifoot, the commercial manager, was seen searching the building for old pieces of string to tie up parcels.

George Riddell went about with his pockets full of handbills, which he left in cabs, in hotels or in railway carriages; he would draw them to the attention of clients who visited his office. Some of the handbills still exist; they advertise the News of the World as the 'Best Family Newspaper, known all over the Globe, enlarged and improved'. The paper claimed to contain the brightest and best reports of the week's news, thrilling series, the latest foreign intelligence, music and the drama, volunteer notes, the latest fashions, society gossip, parliamentary intelligence, plus gardening notes. All for 1d.

The first year's working of the new company showed a profit of £256, but 1894–5's profit of £1,666 was promptly wiped out by a loss in the succeeding year of £2,500, and although 1896–7 was the first of a long number of years in which the profits steadily rose, even after six years' trading, there was an adverse balance of nearly £5,000. These were the lean years, but in 1897–8, the best year to date, with a profit of just over £2,000, it was decided to declare the first dividend of 5 per cent on the ordinary shares.

In the following year a dividend of 9 per cent was paid and this was increased to 10 per cent twelve months later. In 1901 the whole of the debit balance was written off and the slate was clean. In 1903–4 the net profit so increased that a dividend was declared of 15 per cent free of tax, with a bonus of £1 per share. The anxious days were over.

The circulation battle had also been fought and won. From 51,000 in 1891, the figure increased by 10,000 in the first year, and then by further leaps to nearly 100,000 after the first five years. From then on the advance was astonishing. Three more presses went in before 1904, while more offices in Fleet Street were bought. Then the paper spread to 6 and 8 Bouverie Street. Gradually the present-day newspaper empire was being built.

The News of the World was one of the first newspapers to be mechanically composed, and at little cost. A deal was made with a linotype company, which was persuaded to put fourteen of its machines into the Whitefriars Street premises for nothing. These machines were invaluable, since not only did they set the paper but they also did work for other firms.

The growth of the financial side was staggering. In 1904 there was a reconstruction and a new company was incorporated on 28 July, with a nominal share capital of £200,000, divided into ten thousand ordinary shares of £10 each and ten thousand six per cent cumulative preference shares of £10 each. Riddell emerged with the second largest holding. He had 1,934 ordinary shares and 2,445 preference shares; Jackson held 2,464 and 3,239 and Emsley Carr 518 and 656. Two years later business had been so good that the capital of the company was increased to £300,000 by the creation of ten thousand additional ordinary shares of £10 each. In December, 1912, there was a bonus issue to shareholders of £5 per share on their new shares, and in August 1913 a further bonus of £5, making these ten thousand £10-shares fully paid.

In 1921 it was found possible to make available from profits the amount required to make a further bonus issue of ten thousand ordinary shares of £10 each, fully paid to the holders of ordinary shares, in proportion to their holding. So the process went on, and, as Riddell commented: 'The Bible truthfully says: "Unto him that hath shall be given".'

From the old documents it is clear that Riddell took great care to juggle with the Articles of Association to suit any particular plan of the moment. Scores of alterations, phrased and re-phrased, are carefully noted in his own hand. As the mood suited him, so he would support, or just as easily thwart, those who worked closely with him.

A few minutes would suffice for a general meeting of shareholders. They were never told all that was going on.

But one thing was certain; Riddell was increasing the profits prolifically. They were content and approved the item 'That the agreement between George Allardice Riddell and the News of the World be, and is, hereby confirmed'. Later he had all these records destroyed.

In 1923 Jackson, who had succeeded Lascelles Carr as Chairman, died and Riddell was able to achieve an ambition by being appointed in his place. Jackson's will made Riddell one of his executors and trustees. Though he was a rich man his life had been stormy and, like Riddell, his matrimonial affairs had been difficult. He was at pains, in his last testament, to provide adequately for his children, and, as one of the trustees, it was Riddell's duty to see that these interests were safeguarded.

The problem exercised his mind. Much of Jackson's money was bound up in the newspaper, and if, for some reason, the paper should fail, the children would suffer. The straightforward question to be decided was whether the Jackson trust was overloaded with News of the World shares. After long thought, as solicitor, adviser to the family and one who also knew the state of the paper's finances inside out, Riddell came to the conclusion that it was, and he advised that a large proportion of the Jackson holding be sold, adding that he was prepared to take the shares himself.

An application was made to the High Court and, with the concurrence of the other trustees, (including the Public Trustee), permission was given for this to be done. In Riddell's homely phrase, it was not wise 'that all the Jackson eggs should be in one basket'. So some were removed and placed in Riddell's basket. Any doubt, he said, that he might have had about the paper's finances when he went into court did not materialise, and at the end of 1925 he became both Chairman and principal shareholder. He reflected that, for one who had started in 1891 with a gift of 192 shares for his work as a solicitor in forming the new company, he had done tolerably well.

Two years later he brought about another major

reconstruction of the company's finances, and, in 1929, yet another. Then in 1932 he announced that £300,000 of undivided profits, held in the reserve fund of the company, would be used to pay up the balance outstanding on each ordinary share. This meant that not only were the ordinary shares again fully paid up, but that in fifteen years £11. 10s tax free had been returned on each, and a bonus of nominal value of £40 per share also presented to the shareholders. Within two or three years this nominal £40 became worth more than £60 on the open market.

Riddell's financial triumph was complete. He held over fourteen thousand of the ordinary shares carrying voting power, with the Jacksons holding eight thousand and the Carrs five thousand. His full holding, including first and second preference shares, was worth well over £1,100,000. And they had cost him nothing.

'There was no doubt he was a financial genius,' Harry Aldridge, who started as an errand boy at the paper and eventually became Chairman, told me when we spent hours discussing this remarkable man. 'We all feared him, but had to acknowledge that he was one of the biggest men in the Street.'

# 7  Crime and Punishment

By 1906 the character of the paper had emerged and settled down. Chief interest lay in the subjects in the following order: politics, sport, news of the day, crime and, lastly, divorce cases (not unhumorously headed Marital Woe).

A great deal of space was also given to competitions with big money prizes and to life-stories of the famous and infamous. There was a service called 'Missing Relatives' by which hundreds of people were traced; and a column called 'Unclaimed Money' which resulted in millions of pounds being received by the rightful owners. Add to these women's fashions and letters (mostly of complaint on innumerable subjects) and you had the Edwardian formula for a successful Sunday newspaper. It reflected the interests of all ordinary men and women at that time — crime, sport, sex, news, a gamble and something light-hearted like a story and a song. It was never highbrow, facetious or too clever and, above all, identified itself so closely with its readers that it became part of family life. The slogan *Good old News of the World*, posted over the countryside, expressed exactly its readers' feelings.

There were some critics but Riddell could be as tough as they were. To any who commented on the extent of the news from the courts he would say: 'We may publish the crime, but we also record the punishment.'

He was even shorter with the head of a brewery who tackled him on the golf course. 'Don't these reports increase the amount of crime?' asked the innocent. 'Certainly not,' thundered Riddell. 'We fight crime and your bloody beer causes it.'

In quieter vein he would point out, truthfully, that the

44

paper reported the facts. It did not invent the news and he would ask: 'Should we ignore the facts? Should we pretend that crime does not exist?'

On the circulation side he appointed thousands of direct agents throughout the country who were not necessarily connected with the newspaper trade during the week. These appointments had the double effect of opening up new channels of sale and stimulating the newsagents. He was frequently in conflict with the law over these Sunday sales, which were partly controlled by an Act of Parliament passed in the reign of Charles II. Wherever possible he championed the cause of the newspaper sellers.

Bob Berry, the assistant editor, introduced a down-at-heel actor whom he said was just the man to go around appointing agents for the paper. Riddell told the actor to appoint an agent in a village in Surrey to see what he could do. When the actor asked what sort of agent he should get, Riddell replied 'Get the village idiot; no-one will prosecute him. Everybody has great sympathy for the village idiot.' Off went the actor. Next day he was back. 'Well,' snapped Riddell in his usual style, 'did you get the agent?' 'No sir, I couldn't find anyone silly enough.' Riddell's comment, 'bloody fool', was one of his favourite expressions. A substantial shareholder stupid enough to ask what would happen if Riddell lost all his money received the reply: 'I'll soon get some more from another bloody fool!'

One day, however, he overstepped himself. Taking off his receiver he growled a number into the telephone. It happened to be a new operator, who asked who was speaking. 'Don't you know, you bloody fool?' The operator complained to his union: he was new, he had no idea who was calling and he didn't intend to be spoken to like that. The union demanded an apology under threat of refusing to print the paper, and it took all the persuasive skill of the manager, with promises that he would look into the complaint and do something about it, to get the wheels turning.

The moment printing had begun he went round to the Post Office to telephone Riddell so that he could not be overheard. Riddell told him to come and see him and the manager explained about the complaint and how near they had been to having no paper. 'Me, rude to a telephone operator!' said Riddell. 'Ridiculous! What expression am I supposed to have used? ... *Bloody fool?* Those are words I never use!'

As a party piece one sub-editor used to give a very fair imitation of Riddell's voice. He would ring up someone else in the office, adopt Riddell's tone and enjoy the quavering reply. But soon everybody was wise to his performance. One day the sports editor's telephone rang, and when a shattering rocket in the Riddell manner came from the ear-piece, he wasn't going to be caught. So, with his friends standing round, he bellowed back: 'And you're a bloody fool, too.' Laughter filled the office, but suddenly froze: the joker, whom everybody thought was on the other end of the line, walked into the room.

John Hinchcliffe, an assistant editor and legal man, claimed he was the last member of the editorial staff to have a serious conversation with Riddell. 'Who's that?' demanded Riddell on the telephone. 'Hinchcliffe.' 'And who the bloody hell are you?' bellowed the proprietor.

The subject of his own health, or that of others, never failed to arouse Riddell's interest. He advised one of his staff to go and see his own doctor. Next day he wanted to know what the doctor had said and, on being told that the doctor had recommended more exercise said: 'Quite right, you must have a horse.' It mattered not that there were no facilities for keeping a horse at a modest suburban home. A horse was sent round and tethered to the front gate.

His reactions could never be predicted. One winter evening he said to one of his staff: 'You need some fresh air, get in my car and I'll give you a lift home.' Riddell, as always in his open Rolls-Royce, was wrapped up to the ears in a fur-collared overcoat while his companion shivered in a jacket. As they drove Riddell began to talk on a variety of subjects until they eventually saw some lights in the distance. 'That's High Wycombe station,' said Riddell, 'get out and get yourself a train.' The poor man lived on the other side of London.

'You could never be sure of your welcome,' said Harry Aldridge. 'I was with Riddell at his house at Queen Anne's Gate in London, when the maid came in and announced: "Mr So-and-so is here". It was somebody of importance. Riddell didn't look up, nor did he notice that the visitor had entered the room. "To hell with Mr So-and-so", he growled. Then, turning round, "How did I know you were creeping about?" '

A difficult father of the chapel once mixed up his own money with the union members' funds and, with the auditor due, had to find £200 quickly. Riddell thought it would be a good thing to give the FOC the money and thereafter have him in his pocket, and he only dropped the idea when the dangerous side of the intrigue was pointed out to him. However, he agreed to see the FOC at his house. Next day Riddell reported the conversation to Aldridge. 'I should like to have seen his face,' remarked Riddell, 'when I told him what I thought of him.' 'But surely you did see his face?' 'No, I kept him outside the front door and made him speak to me through the letter-box! I'm convinced that that man is a germ carrier.' Terrified of illness, Riddell had quite irrationally got it into his head, that the FOC carried some foul disease and refused to go near him. The story conjures up an intriguing scene — the FOC on his knees outside the front door shouting through the letter-box and Riddell, crouching on the mat inside, growling his replies.

Meanwhile the Sunday newspaper battle for circulation continued — the race to sell a million copies of one issue before any other paper. Lloyd's Sunday News produced a giant poster showing a yacht race with the leader about to cross the finishing line, with the caption reading 'rounding the million mark'. The News of the World was at that time nowhere in sight, but its competitors underestimated it. Coming from behind, the outsider won the race. In 1904, 700,000 copies were sold each week; by 1906 it was a million; the two million mark was topped in 1914, and a million more put on by 1920. In 1945 it topped eight million.

While Riddell was engrossed in the business side, Emsley Carr, the Editor, was improving and brightening up the pages. He introduced a new feature for which the paper became famous — the first popular songs printed with words and music. Every weekend, up and down the country, families gathered round the piano, with mother playing and father singing. One of the first was *Our Lodger's such a Nice Young Man*, as sung on the halls by Miss Vesta Victoria. The songs were remembered by many of the old-time variety artists, Gracie Fields among them. For fifty years the paper made all Britain sing.

In the advertisement columns of an issue of 1902 a pair of boots was offered free, if the purchaser would buy a suit for 27s. 6d. Fashions included the Princess Gown for the eighteen-inch waist. A woman received seven years for killing her maid; Dan Leno was at the Canterbury; Sir Henry Irving delighted the West End. Someone solemnly declared that, with the increase of the number of omnibuses in London, ladies were ousting men from what used to be their proper preserve — the seats on the top. 'Fathers,' demanded a bold advertisement, 'will you allow your wife to carry a heavy baby when we supply prams for one shilling weekly?'

No opportunity to build up the circulation was missed. Riddell would ride on vans going to the stations, dropping a tip here and there, ensuring that all went smoothly. He even started special newspaper trains, hiring them direct from the railways and letting other newspapers come in, at a price. If his paper was aboard off went the train; too bad if the others were late. But if his paper was late the train had to wait. He got enough money from the other papers to pay the bill. His went free.

When the paper badly needed a new series of articles, one of the ideas that came to the rescue was called 'The earthly footsteps of the Man of Galilee'. Thousands of extra copies were sold. 'I was never so astonished,' said Riddell. 'I had no idea that our readers knew who the Man of Galilee was.'

Another idea that sent sales rocketing was the limerick competition, in which competitors were required to add the last line to this sort of verse:

> There was a young lady of Bow
> Who got sick of the weather, and so
> When it rained in July
> She said, 'Oh, my eye,
> . . . . . . . . . . . . . '

and one of the winning lines was 'I'd wear bloomers, but people stare so'. The entry fee was 6d. and each week £4,000 was divided among the winning competitors.

Riddell was a great believer in promotion. A member of his staff was in the Law Courts Branch of Lloyds Bank when he saw Riddell come in, walk round the spacious hall, visiting each writing table in turn, and then go out. The observer walked over to one of the tables where he found, tucked under the blotter, a handbill announcing: *The News of the World* — *best Sunday newspaper*. Few proprietors did that.

During the railway strike of 1911, papers were distributed by road: steam-driven buses, horse-drawn vans, small cars, open cars with improvised platforms, were all pressed into service. A motley fleet stretched the whole length of Bouverie Street and Temple Avenue, along the Embankment almost to Waterloo Bridge, and along Fleet Street to the Law Courts.

Steam-driven vehicles, intended for short journeys in and around London, had to do trips of three hundred miles. Most of them made it, although a few limped back days afterwards. It was a triumph of improvisation. Valuable lessons were learned for the future and when the railwaymen came out on strike again in 1919 and 1926, it was known how to cope with the situation. Imagine a straw-hatted reporter clinging to the platform of a steam-waggon, bound from London to Newcastle! But they got through and when the big vehicles reached their various destinations, a swarm of small ones was waiting to take the papers on.

'My own task lay in the West Country where we printed on the machines of the Western Mail,' records Stanley Baker, a director for many years. 'From Cardiff we took a supply of papers to Bristol by sea, hiring two trawlers. Fog in the channel made it impossible to get up the Severn to Bristol, so we disembarked at Avonmouth where vehicles were waiting to rush the papers into West Country towns.'

The dock strike of 1912 was an opportunity to show the paper's concern for the wives and children of men coming home without pay packets. Dozens of vans, each drawn by two horses, were hired and formed up near the office to distribute free bread to hundreds of families in the East End of London. On the sides of the vans were attached contents bills which read: 'Look out for the *free bread carts* on Saturday mornings.' Forty tons of bread were delivered, including a van-load which arrived at Greenhithe in the east of London, just as the people were kneeling on the Green to pray for food: manna had arrived — not from heaven, but from the News of the World.

One day Riddell arrived at the office with a complicated machine on a tripod, which, when played, made a frightening noise. He first commanded that it should be played in the hall and then on the first floor; he then surprised everybody by instructing a young reporter to hire a horse and wagonette, put the machine in it and play it in the streets. 'I want you to get summoned,' he said, 'and I want the instrument played in court.'

'Mine was not to reason why,' said the reporter to me many years later. 'I did as I was told. Actually I had the greatest difficulty in getting myself summoned. The police were far too good-natured. Eventually, when I made myself an intolerable nuisance, a police sergeant took my name and I was summoned for causing an obstruction. So far, so good. Riddell was delighted. The day of the case came and I duly appeared. I was fined £1 or seven days. The office paid. And Riddell was furious because the magistrate would not allow the machine (it was the first gramophone) to be played in court.'

What was the point of this stunt? The young man didn't know, but there always was a point when Riddell decided to do something: this time it was because he was acting as solicitor to the gramophone company that wanted the instrument advertised.

'Make no mistake,' said Aldridge, 'Riddell never did anything unless the move had been nicely calculated, and usually the result benefited his pocket. He used to say: "Every man has a price." '

Another stunt was a competition to find hidden treasure. Tubes holding fifty golden sovereigns were hidden at various places and clues were given in the paper. With the fifty sovereigns would be a note to say that if the finder came to the office he would receive another £50. Thousands of people spent their weekends searching for the treasure. But Riddell came to dislike the competition: 'It seems to me,' he said darkly to the reporters, 'that some of these sovereigns are being found before they are hidden.' His faith in others, certainly in reporters, was not great.

# 8  Ten Fags for 2d.

Fleet Street was a gay place in the 'nineties. Newspapermen worked hard for small pay but beer was 1d. a pint and cigarettes were ten for 2d. Cyclists, with ten quires of papers slung over their shoulders, would thread their way through the horse-drawn traffic.

One of the popular music-hall songs referred to the Hidden Treasure Competition:

I'm looking for the hidden treasure,
Digging little holes in the ground,
Picking up the walk with the toasting-fork,
Looking for the fifty pounds.

There was a Popular Barmaids Competition for which coupons were printed in the paper, and the barmaid who got the most votes won a bicycle. The bike, decorated with ribbons, was hung in the bar and the News of the World staff, it was said — no doubt with some truth — became very friendly with the barmaids.

Bob Berry was responsible for many of the paper's stunts. He was one of the great characters of Fleet Street. Old-timers of the music-hall spoke of him with near reverence, for Berry 'made' many of them. One story had it that nothing happened in the theatre without his consent. Another that Scotland Yard invariably rang him up before making an arrest. Hardly likely! On a summer's day Berry would wear a suit of tussore-silk, and that's how I first saw him. On the way to the office he would hire a cab which trailed along behind him if he felt like walking, and stopped for him whenever he wished to ride. He would pay the cabbie off at the end of the day. It wasn't all that expensive and the office paid. Bohemians abounded in The Street in those days.

The drama critic was seldom seen out of top hat and frock coat, but he could shin down a rainpipe at the back of the office with greater agility than a tax-collector could climb the front staircase. In the old Whitefriars Street building, the Editor sat in the attic, and the only room to boast a carpet was that of the general manager. Aldridge always kept that carpet.

A Russian student was employed to translate intriguing stories from newspapers printed in foreign languages. The student supplied one story a week and Berry had the task of writing it up, but much to his annoyance he discovered that the student was being paid far more than himself. To overcome this he bumped up his expense account. However there was a snag; the general manager — who was once known to have questioned a bill containing the item 'one orange' — watched expenses with an eagle eye. Berry's claim 'entertaining police' was too much and he refused to sign.

Berry went to Riddell and luck was on his side, for Riddell had just attended a conference at which the Commissioner of Police had voiced a fear that newspapermen were paying policemen for information. On behalf of the Press, he solemnly declared that newspapers did not stoop to bribery. When told what Berry's expenses referred to, Riddell was aghast: 'I don't want to know anything about them. Take them away.' And to the general manager: 'Sign them, sign them. How dare you trouble me with a matter of this sort?' Berry had scored again.

In his own handwriting, Dr Buck Ruxton wrote an exclusive confession to the double murder for which he was hanged. The confession had been signed before the trial, placed in a sealed envelope and handed to the Editor. It came as a great surprise, the Editor said, when he opened the envelope after the trial since he had had no idea that it contained a confession — he just bought it 'on spec.' The money paid for it was used for Buxton's defence. What would the Press Council say today? That confession was framed and had a place in my room.

When newspaper gift schemes arrived, the paper went along with them, as did their rivals, but only for a time. The Editor declared: 'Money which should be spent in the better management and production of a paper, improving the conditions under which the journalist works, is now being thrown away. Is there anyone who will admit that a free distribution of washing machines, pyjamas, pillow cases and silk stockings to capture any and everybody is consonant with the traditions of British journalism?' The paper dropped this idea and the readers' free insurance. I am sorry to see these free gifts have returned for the view at 30 Bouverie Street in my day, was that a newspaper was worth the money charged for it.

Joe Hopcraft who joined the staff in 1897 as an office boy at 6s. 6d. a week, became sports editor and put in fifty years' service. His contributors included all the great champions of the day. 'We put professional golf on its feet,' he claimed. 'In the early 1900s the income of professional golfers was pretty small, coming mainly from clubs and teaching. A winner of the Open Championship received £50. We then stepped in with £250.' A top golfer would hardly be impressed today; but then it was something.

It was in Bouverie Street that the paper's amazing growth took place. In April 1927 it announced that it had been decided 'in consequence of an ever-increasing circulation, to extend the premises. The new building would be a handsome addition to London's architectural treasures. Nothing would be lacking to facilitate the work of all departments. It would occupy the greater part of Bouverie Street and Whitefriars Street, extending over five acres, of which one acre would be devoted to the machine halls. The plans had been prepared after considerable study on the Continent, throughout Canada and the United States.'

54

Each Sunday four million copies of the paper would be printed on the finest battery of printing presses the world had ever seen — sixty-six units in all, with a combined capacity of 1¼ million copies per hour. Each issue would require 500 tons of paper, 16,000 lb of ink and, to tie up the parcels, 70 miles of string. It was distributed by over forty thousand newsagents.

Over the next two years the new building took shape. A notice was erected in the street apologising for the noise made by the builders, and asking for the indulgence of other workers and passers-by — an act of courtesy that was duly commented upon by Fleet Street columnists.

Riddell was greatly pleased as he saw the new building going up, though there were moments when the cost gave him qualms.

He walked around watching the decorators at work, listening to the chatter of the Italians engaged on the flooring. In a rare sociable mood, he addressed one: 'And from what part of Italy do you come?' The worker looked at him: 'Don't be bleeding silly, guv'ner, I'm from bloody 'Oxton.' A delighted smile crossed Riddell's face: 'Well, it's a pleasure to hear the King's English!'

That was one of the happier Riddell stories. Others are less cheerful. A lad came dashing down the stairs as Riddell was walking up. He stopped the boy: 'Do you work here?' 'No,' replied the boy, 'I've just delivered a message.' Then Riddell asked one of the odd questions with which he loved to floor people: 'Tell me, where does rubber come from?' The bright-looking boy gave the correct answer. 'Like to work here?' queried Riddell. 'Yes, sir.' So the boy was taken on. Soon afterwards various articles and cash began to disappear and a trap was laid, and the new boy was caught and quietly dismissed. For years after that the question, 'Where does rubber come from?' was the joke of the office.

By 1930 the new building was finished. No name was given to it, though a competition was run among the staff with a prize of £1 for the best suggestion. It remained simply 30 Bouverie Street. As the staff moved in, the conversation not unnaturally went back to the 'good old days' of the 'nineties. Then there were only sixty employees and they all went on the first annual outing to the Bell, at Taplow. By 1930 there were more than one thousand on the payroll. It was to grow many times larger.

# 9  Corset in Cabinet

The breakdown in his health, which had earlier threatened Riddell, now became a reality. Urgently summoned to the office, his doctor found him collapsed from a combination of overwork, nervous exhaustion and strain, plus insufficient attention to regular meals and lack of sleep.

This time the doctor did the talking and Riddell listened. He was killing himself, and not slowly. If he continued this way he would be dead in a matter of months. The choice lay with him. 'You've said all this bloody nonsense before,' said Riddell. Reaching for his hat, the doctor replied 'And you can get someone else to treat you'. With that he walked out.

Riddell was frightened. His first decision was to enter a nursing home and regain his health by rest and ordered living. While in bed he made another important decision. He would cut his work in half by giving up as a solicitor, though he would maintain a financial interest and continue to take out a practising certificate. It might still come in useful. He would also get out into the open air and take more exercise.

His mind made up and the decision taken, he didn't go back on it. He told a friend: 'One day I was walking down the street when I suddenly said to myself: 'What am I getting out of life? Why am I working so hard? What good does it do me? I must stop it at once. There are other things in life besides work; worthwhile things. I must enjoy them while I can.' From that moment I gave up practising as a solicitor. I began to play golf; I bought a motor car, drove through the countryside, and began to enjoy myself.'

To others he spoke of his strength of mind in giving up smoking. 'I was travelling by train,' he said. 'It was a long, all-night journey. I desperately needed a smoke. I had my cigars with me but couldn't find a match. There was nobody else in the carriage. I sat there and cursed. 'Suddenly I noticed the flame of the acetylene globe in the roof of the carriage [this was before the days of electricity in trains]. It gave me an idea. I smashed the glass globe, lit my cigar from the flame, leaned back and enjoyed it. While I was doing so I began to reflect; if my desire to smoke drives me to do a thing like that it has far too great a hold on me. I'll give it up — and at once. I opened the carriage window, threw out the cigar and my cigar case after it.' While telling the story he didn't seem to notice that the ash from his cigarette was spilling down his waistcoat.

What was he to turn to? The events of 1906 provided the answer; a political upheaval. A headline on 28 January gives the clue: 'Liberals sweep the board clean. Record series of victories.' The News of the World assured readers that 'the accession to power of a party composed of plain and sensible Englishmen need not frighten the oldest of old ladies'. It went on to notice the arrival of the Labour Party in these words: 'The Mother of Parliaments, the Mother of Senates, has taken to herself a band of democrats fresh from the workshops to take a hand in the work of ruling an Empire. The Vere de Veres and the Toms, Bills and Harrys are, at length in real earnest, partners in Britannia Ltd.'

Riddell knew Asquith and Lloyd George. The former was a barrister whom he had frequently briefed, and Lloyd George a Welsh solicitor to whom Lascelles Carr had introduced him in Cardiff.

Lloyd George interested him a great deal. They had much in common: they were about the same age (Lloyd George was born on 17 January 1863, two years earlier than Riddell); Lloyd George's father, like Riddell's, died when he was a child and an uncle provided for his education; before he went into politics, Lloyd George had also chosen the law for his career and he, too, had known hard and difficult years as a struggling solicitor. He was articled in 1879 and took his first certificate in 1884, not so many years before Riddell. In 1900 as a rising young Liberal MP, Lloyd George was spending most of his time in London and the two men formed a friendship important to both of them.

Riddell planned his new life. Now, instead of rushing off to his office in the morning, he took his doctor's advice and rested in bed attending to papers. Next, he would have his car brought round by his chauffeur and was driven off to Walton Heath to play golf. He usually lunched there, and afterwards was driven to his office in Bouverie Street.

The top flat at 1 Portland Place, which he had occupied for years, was now hardly suitable. He needed somewhere more in keeping with his greater stature. His next move was to a beautiful house in Queen Anne's Gate, which he leased from Christ's Hospital. His wife helped him to furnish it with great elegance and engaged a staff to run the establishment in style. Riddell could afford to sit back and reflect that he had arrived.

Motoring enabled him to take plenty of fresh air — cars were open to the weather then — which he felt was essential for his health. His first car was a chain-driven Rolls-Royce. Anyone travelling with him had to stand the buffeting of wind and rain, which he enjoyed. His huge overcoat buttoned up to the top, a hat jammed on his head, he would undertake long journeys by night or day without a qualm.

Once, driving back from Walton Heath with a bishop as a passenger, the car had to brake violently to avoid another vehicle. Both cars stopped and Riddell, in a towering rage, stood up and cursed the other driver. When his not inconsiderable supply of strong language was exhausted, he shouted: 'And if I didn't have a bloody bishop with me I'd tell you exactly what I thought of you.'

Annoyed at being held up in traffic, he bought a police whistle and, urging his chauffeur to higher speeds, he would stand up in the back blowing furiously to clear the way. A horse-drawn van blocked his path. Driving close behind it, he belaboured the black mackintosh curtains of the van with his walking stick until the van driver moved off, to the accompaniment of whacks and curses heard the length of Bouverie Street. 'Get out of my way,' he roared at a van driver on Vauxhall Bridge. 'What's the matter with you, Guy Fawkes. Want all the road?' came the rejoinder. 'Yes,' shouted Riddell, 'if you had it you wouldn't bloody well know what to do with it.'

Golf took a great hold on him. He played four or five days a week at Walton Heath and, under the eagle eye of James Braid, the famous professional of the day, became a reasonable player. As a concession to sporting clothes, Riddell would wear tweeds on the course, but he was never seen without his stiff, high-winged collar. He talked to Lloyd George about golf. It was essential for a cabinet minister to keep fit and strong, he said. This was the way to take exercise in a most convenient and enjoyable form. The fresh air at Walton Heath was invigorating. Besides, Lloyd George could relax there, discuss political problems among friends who could be trusted; it was an escape from the pressure of everyday affairs. Lloyd George agreed. Whenever he wanted to play, Riddell's car was always ready to take him to the course.

If Lloyd George wished to entertain friends in the evening, or to dine quietly and unobtrusively, the house in Queen Anne's Gate was always available. And by now Riddell was an extremely good host. The wine was carefully chosen, and there were cigars, brandy, and the best whisky. But Riddell himself seldom took a drink, which he said was a loosener of tongues. His role was to listen and to record. Soon he started his famous diaries. Each night he would write on lined sheets of foolscap, which were carefully locked away. Only parts of these diaries have been published. The author wished to make certain that everyone he discussed would be dead by the time their secrets were revealed, and the full, unexpurgated versions are in the British Museum and will not be available to the public until 1984, fifty years after Riddell's death.

Riddell asked his wife, the only person he could trust to dispose of them as he required, solemnly to promise that, with the exception of the diaries, all his papers would be burnt; not a scrap was to be left. The other papers he was anxious about were all gathered up in one room in his office in Bouverie Street and taken by lorry to a public incinerator. There were three loads. The confidential clerk saw the papers burnt and then reported to Lady Riddell that his master's instructions had been carried out.

So intent was Riddell on preserving his secrets that many of the newspaper's records were destroyed. Pages containing his name were even removed from the minutes. Few men can have taken so much trouble to cover their tracks.

What was Lloyd George's attitude to this extraordinary character? In his early London days he found Riddell useful in many ways: he appreciated his influence as a newspaperman, and he found him shrewd and sound in judgement. Riddell was also a mine of information about all sorts and sizes of public men, whatever their walk of life. He knew many secrets; he could rattle the skeletons in the cupboard. The 'anonymous' author of *Makers of the New World, by One Who Knows Them* wrote of him:

> No incident is too small for him to notice, no trivial fact escapes his alert mind. Everyone and everything concerns him and contributes to his interest in life and human nature. He probes and prises to find out the why and the wherefore of this and that, and he will take immense trouble to satisy himself as to the governing factors, the interests, in fact the smallest details in the lives of the people with whom he comes into contact.

The writer was Frances Stevenson, Lloyd George's confidential secretary and mistress, who became his second wife. She told me of the friendship between the two men.

Riddell belonged to no political party, and he could often

find out things Lloyd George wanted to know about the other side. He was a great comfort to the man who became Chancellor of the Exchequer and the great war-time Prime Minister. Whenever Lloyd George was worried or overworked, Riddell was always there at his elbow. 'The car is ready; a round of golf would do you good.' Or 'Dinner is ready at my house.' Or 'Why not get away from it all for a bit? I've arranged everything.' He placed not only Walton Heath, but many other country residences at Lloyd George's disposal.

Lloyd George told Frances Stevenson that Riddell got as much out of it as he did, and he was right. Because of their association, Riddell was able to contribute the best-informed column in British journalism. He knew what was going on in Lloyd George's innermost circle.

Not many newspaper columnists have the opportunity to entertain a cabinet minister three or four times a week, either at golf or at their private houses. The information Riddell obtained, not all for publication, was of great value when shrewdly used. And Riddell was shrewd.

He also wanted a peerage. To a self-made man it would place a seal on his achievements for all to see. It would be the complete answer to those who, in his boyhood, thought of him and dealt with him as the poor relation.

When Lloyd George moved to 11 Downing Street, Riddell commented after a visit:

> The furniture and appointments in the Chancellor's house are rather a scratch lot, got together by the Office of Works. Lloyd George told me that Sir William Harcourt, who was sensitive to cold, had all the windows in the library sealed up with brown paper and that, notwithstanding this, he used to sit working in his fur-lined overcoat. The dining-room, by the way, is built on what were formerly the stables. This was done in Mr Gladstone's time.

So the newspaper boss sized up the Chancellor's apartments.

By 1908 Riddell and Lloyd George were constant companions. That year they exchanged Christmas gifts; for the Chancellor a gold watch and chain, and for Riddell a gold cigarette case. Lloyd George was also thinking about building a house at Criccieth in Wales, and he and Riddell spent some time looking over the plans. The price was to be £1,200, which was all Lloyd George could afford. Riddell was helpful.

As Chancellor the only way that Lloyd George could go on enjoying his golf was to have a house at Walton Heath. There was far more fresh air at Walton than in the narrow confines of Downing Street. It was important that he should be fit to run the affairs of the nation.

It so happened that Riddell had bought a lot of ground at Walton — on unusually advantageous terms — and it was not difficult to make a plot available for Lloyd George. As for the cost of building, this was well within Riddell's means. He wrote to a friend: 'Lloyd George is very anxious to take possession of the house I am building for him at Walton, so that he may spend Christmas there. He asked me to hurry up the builders.'

Suffragettes tried to blow up the house with a home-made bomb, an incident that made Riddell extremely angry since he was a secret contributor to the suffragette funds. Not that he believed in their ideas, it was — or so he thought — simply an investment. Everything had to be an investment. For Lloyd George, the Walton Heath house was a haven of seclusion during the anxious years of World War I. Many were the secret callers — statesmen, generals, businessmen, Irish leaders, princes; and Frances Stevenson.

Such was the Chancellor's confidence in him that Riddell was consulted, behind the scenes, in the great Marconi scandal of 1913 which threatened to wreck the careers of the Liberal leaders. Lloyd George and others, had bought shares in the American Marconi Company at a time when the Post Office was discussing the terms of a contract with the British Marconi Company.

'The two concerns were separate,' wrote Riddell. 'There could in fairness be no accusation of anything beyond indiscretion. The matter became the subject of an enquiry by a Committee of the House of Commons. The majority acquitted Lloyd George, and the House of Commons replied to the Opposition's attacks by a vote of confidence.'

The three friends — Lloyd George, Rufus Isaacs, (afterwards Lord Reading, Lord Chief Justice and Viceroy of India) and Riddell — spent long hours in consultation at Walton Heath and Queen Anne's Gate, where they were able to speak freely. Riddell was also able to sound the Conservatives, and he was able to tell Lloyd George that Bonar Law, the Conservative leader, took the view that there was no corruption, but some imprudence.

Riddell now held a remarkable position, described by some as 'an extra member of the Liberal Cabinet'. His wealth and shrewdness had contributed; so had Walton Heath Golf Club; so had his paper.

He carried out many undercover actions. In 1913, for example, Westminster was excited by a police raid on a brothel in Piccadilly. Papers found on the premises contained the names of some of the patrons of the establishment: they were important men. Riddell worked fast. 'Malicious rumours,' he wrote. 'The rumours are a pack of lies but they have engendered much resentment and bad feeling.' He squashed the rumours and many were indebted to him.

Riddell found that important people sought his company more than ever as they began to recognise that to have his ear was a long way towards having the ear of the Chancellor. Golfing parties at Walton Heath were now important social occasions. The Prince of Wales and his brothers went there, as did Churchill, even though he regarded the game purely as an aid to conversation. Bernard Darwin has recalled those days at Walton Heath in his biography of James Braid.

Riddell was by this time a person of great authority, indeed of supreme authority, at Walton. He wasted no time; the moment we reached the club the bowler hat, which he invariably wore in the car, was exchanged for a cap. James Braid was ready in the shop and off we went. Similarly, when the day's golf was over the bowler was instantly reassumed, and, in less than no time, we were being frozen on Banstead Downs on the way back to London. He was a remarkable golfer, in that he was inclined to talk continuously on all sorts of subjects during the round and yet keep his mind on the match, which he very properly liked to win.

I have in my mind a vivid picture of him putting with his right foot drawn far back while he leered, or, perhaps I should say, scowled at the ball over his left shoulder. It looked uncomfortable, but he was a good holer of a nasty putt at a pinch … Walton Heath had a decidedly political atmosphere. Eminent statesmen and newspaper editors and proprietors were often to be seen there, and they may have even spoken more or less off their guard, knowing that by the discreet James they would never be repeated.

There was golf on Sundays, not 'the thing' sixty years ago, and in the evening Lloyd George and Riddell would stand round the piano and sing hymns while Frances played. Every night Riddell recorded what Lloyd George had said. On 26 June 1913, for example, he wrote:

Talked with Lloyd George regarding domestic relations. He said: 'I don't think it good for a man to be on his wife's leading strings. There are some men who spend all their spare time with their wives; motor with them, play golf with them. I think this is bad for both parties. It is better for a man to spend a considerable part of his leisure with men. It is essential to cultivate the male point of view.'

At the start of the 1914 war the whole relationship between Press and Government was at an experimental stage. Kitchener neither understood the Press and its importance to the nation, nor wished to have any dealings with it. He and others were to learn and Riddell who was admirably suited to the task, taught them. He knew all the political leaders and was a figure of importance in the newspaper world while his training as a solicitor and experience in negotiation had taught him the value of caution. He had no easy task for while the Press clamoured for news about the war, the Cabinet and the Services were chary of giving it. Somehow Riddell managed to satisfy both. When the imminence of war with Germany was discussed, he drafted the first secret and confidential Note to Editors on a piece of paper he picked up in the room.

It was largely because of Riddell that newspapers were allowed to send their own reporters to the Front, which is today regarded as a matter of routine, but was then a sensational step forward. Riddell kept his post as the link between newspapers and the Government throughout the war and at the peace conference which followed.

He went to see Kitchener, a martinet of the first order, about arrangements for war correspondents. All was not moving smoothly, but Kitchener either could not or would not see him. Riddell stationed himself outside Kitchener's room, telling an official that he would wait all day if need be. And so he did, from early morning till late at night, without leaving his post for a meal. Eventually Kitchener left to go home to bed and, as he walked out of his room, he found Riddell at his elbow. That was his style.

An entry in Riddell's diary for 20 May 1915 reveals Churchill in a mood of blackest despair after the Dardanelles, saying to Riddell: 'I am the victim of a political intrigue. I am finished.' But Riddell who had recognised

Churchill's greatness, replied: 'No, not finished at forty, with your powers.'

Throughout the war he was at the side of Lloyd George. It was faithful service and he was rewarded in a gratifying way. The citation read: 'Jan. 1st, 1918. Baronet, Sir George Riddell, Director of the News of the World, George Newnes Ltd, and other publishing firms. Born in 1865, and admitted a solicitor in 1888. Knighted in 1909. As Vice-Chairman of the Newspaper Proprietors' Association and Newspaper Society during the last three difficult years he had rendered important services in focusing correspondence between the Government and the Press.'

When the news came through officially — he had long known that the honour was on its way — Riddell turned to one of his secretaries and exclaimed: 'And next I shall have a peerage.' He did, too. He also changed the motto he had at first selected — 'Money is Power' — to 'Knowledge is Power'. There are more ways than one of interpreting those words, and Riddell had great knowledge of many things and of many people.

His bizarre sense of humour continued. Invited to 10 Downing Street to give his views on the paper shortage, he gave a demonstration. 'This, gentlemen,' he said, 'is an article typical of many being sold to ladies in shops every day. Is the paper necessary?' Carefully he unwrapped a parcel, piling the numerous pieces of wrapping in front of him. By the time he had finished, Riddell could barely peer over the top but at last he brandished aloft the unwrapped article — a corset. A moment of shocked silence was broken by Lloyd George's shout of laughter. Slapping Riddell on the back he declared: 'That's the first time I've seen a corset in the Cabinet Room!' There were those who doubted it.

# 10  Rift with Lloyd George

After World War I, Lloyd George suggested that Riddell went to Paris with him to look after the British Press during the Peace Conference. It was there that the first seeds of friction between the two were sown. The Prime Minister, with the world at his feet, acclaimed on all sides, was in no mood to be criticised by anyone. When convinced that his policy was right, he liked to be surrounded by men whole-heartedly behind him. Occasionally, his greatness was obscured by a pettiness that was not in his true nature, but that was not altogether surprising, for the difficulties of the Peace Conference were many and great and the demands upon him were immense, and while he was so engaged, his critics at home were getting at him behind his back.

In these circumstances, Lloyd George was not at all pleased when Riddell could not see eye to eye with him on his pro-Greek policy. In matters of foreign affairs he did not wish to listen to Riddell's views. But Riddell had also grown in stature.

Millionaire, peer, known to the greatest, he felt that the man he had helped for years should listen to what he had to say. He believed that Lloyd George was wrong in supporting the Greeks against the Turks. When the Prime Minister discovered this, he suspected that other influences, particularly the French, had been at work on Riddell. There is no doubt that Riddell's vanity had been touched by the French politicians, who had made a great fuss of him at the Peace Conference and even given him a decoration.

When Riddell attempted to influence Lloyd George on the Greek issue, however, he met stubborn, even bitter, resistance. Said Lloyd George on one occasion after Riddell had left: 'Does he think he can teach me my business?' All was not the same between the two men who had gone through so much together, but the quarrel had yet to burst into flame. Riddell was not unduly upset when Lloyd George called him 'Pasha Riddell' because he supported the Turks, and only the closest friends noticed the critical note that had crept into the relationship.

At Gairloch in 1921 the long-threatened quarrel came to a head. It had been a difficult year for Lloyd George. The Irish were being particularly troublesome and Lloyd George called the Cabinet up to Scotland to consider the Government's position — not a popular move with those who had to make the long journey. The Prime Minister was suffering from severe toothache and his temper was raw, and this was the moment when Riddell chose to bandy words with him about a statement to the Press. Those at dinner that night recall that both men were in a savage mood. Strong words were used and when Lloyd George called him a traitor, Riddell left the room, saying to a friend: 'The little man has become impossible.'

But they continued to meet. Riddell's skin was thick and, in 1921, it was by no means certain that Lloyd George's day was done, although the writing may have been on the wall. But, as usual, Riddell was taking no chances. In November of that year he went to the Disarmament Conference at Washington at the special request of Mr Balfour. It was the first time he had shown any inclination to leave Lloyd George's side, and Balfour, Foreign Secretary in the Coalition Government, was one of the Conservative leaders. The Prime Minister watched with cynical interest. Next followed Anglo-French talks at Cannes, and it was here that Riddell arranged for LG and Briand, the French Premier, to play golf. They were photographed together and Briand was highly criticised. It was assumed in Paris that he had fallen under LG's influence, and his Government fell.

On his return to England, The Times paid a warm tribute to Riddell's work and the French papers commented that M

Poincaré, the new French Premier, should provide himself with a French 'Lord Riddell'. He had become a figure of world importance.

The year 1922 saw the end of the Coalition Government and Bonar Law became Prime Minister. Riddell hurried around, but too late — Beaverbrook was already there. Lloyd George said that Riddell, like a rat, had left the sinking ship; Riddell complained that the Welsh Wizard, who had twisted everyone in turn, had finished by twisting himself.

Lord Beaverbrook thought it foolish that the two old friends should not make up their differences, and arranged for Riddell to call on Lloyd George at his house at Churt in Surrey. The ex-Premier and Frances Stevenson were in the garden when they were told that Lord Riddell had called, and they walked back to the house, their terrier bounding ahead. When they got inside Riddell was glued to a chair, the dog, with teeth bared, defying him to move. Lloyd George thought it a great joke but Riddell was not amused, and he rushed from the house declaring: 'the dog is vicious, like his master.'

After the death of Lloyd George, whom she married in 1943, Frances Stevenson described the remarkable friendship between her husband and Riddell.

Riddell was an arch-cynic. Life had embittered him. He saw an ulterior motive in any action, even by his friends. He admitted it and said that was what life had taught him. Everyone, he said, had his price. Every man was out to gain something.

Riddell saw nothing more in Lloyd George's actions than the popular move; the desire for notoriety. He completely misread him. Even his diaries often fail to note the importance and significance of Lloyd George's work. Because of Riddell's first marriage there was considerable difficulty over his peerage. In fact, only a man of Lloyd George's strength could have pushed it through. Lloyd George told me he had said to the King that he wanted a peerage for Riddell, and that was that. Nevertheless it was a tricky moment.

Lloyd George was extremely trusting, and, amongst friends, spoke his mind freely. Riddell was always there, noting what he said and recording it in his diary. I knew about the diaries and spoke to my husband about them, but Lloyd George just didn't care what Riddell wrote or said about him.

Frances Stevenson described Riddell as a mine of information. He never forgot a face or a fact. As soon as he met anybody he started to find out everything about them; even personal and intimate details. But he never talked about himself. 'Riddell did everything he could to ingratiate himself into Lloyd George's household and would tip the servants handsomely,' she said. 'Naturally they were always glad to see him. But I heard from others that he could be tough, hard and cruel when he wished to be. He never gave anyone credit for high ideals or altruistic motives. He loved to be thought of as the man who knew all the secrets. If not all, he certainly knew many.'

Riddell latterly spent most of his time at Walton Heath Golf Club (he owned 8,300 of the 10,000 shares in the club), where he took over the Dormy House as his home, re-naming it Walton Heath House. Lady Riddell was rarely with him.

Not the least concerned about his personal appearance, he wore old suits, drainpipe trousers baggy at the knees, and into the pockets, placed in front, he would thrust his hands as he walked about in an attitude described as a 'scholarly stoop'. An American reporter wrote that Lord Riddell, a 'shrinking violet', couldn't possibly have visited a first-class tailor for years. This amused Riddell, and the next time he paid his tailor he enclosed the newspaper article.

No-one would have guessed he was rich. His rooms at Walton Heath were small and simply furnished. He slept on a single iron bedstead. His food was simple and he rarely touched alcohol, although when in a gallant mood he would dip a finger into a glass of champagne held by a lady, touch the back of her hand, and press it to his lips, a gesture that went oddly with his character.

With cigars banned by his doctor, he now smoked Turkish cigarettes, using a long slim holder. Later, to his annoyance, even these were forbidden, but his will power was cast iron. It seemed he could always give up anything, except trouble. He enjoyed golf, gambled on the result, and took longer holidays, particularly at Turnberry in Scotland. Usually he took one or two men friends with him; sometimes they were connected with his business interests, sometimes not for their main function was to keep him interested and amused, since he did not care to be alone as he grew older. Sometimes he would say he felt an urge to visit the scenes of his boyhood in Scotland (a fiction he had almost come to believe), and once he pointed out to a companion the house where he was born and the office where he first worked at Duns in Berwickshire. It was quite untrue.

He explained that he was descended from an ancient Scottish family and that his ancestors went back to Robert the Bruce. It was typical of him that he added that his wife came from an illegitimate branch of the same family. He came to have an affection for Scotland that was shared only by Walton Heath, a name he made part of his title, and it was in Scotland and at Walton that he spent his happiest days.

A sidelight on his gruff nature is revealed in his encounter with two young men who drove up in a sports car to the front of the Walton Heath club house, wanting to play a round. Noticing an old man standing there, they asked politely if he knew where the caddy master was. Riddell treated them to a long hard stare before he growled: 'Yes, but he doesn't want any more caddies.'

Riddell was not a successful author. He made millions out

72

of newspapers, but it was as an author that he prided himself. Before his war books appeared, he sent proofs to Lloyd George, saying he hoped nothing he had written would cause him embarrassment. The proofs were returned unopened with a message that, so far as Mr Lloyd George was concerned, Lord Riddell could write what he liked.

One luxury that Riddell did permit himself was a new car every year, the latest Rolls-Royce. Neither his first nor his second chauffeur was overawed by their short-tempered master. The first remembered driving Riddell to Sidney Street to see the police and troops shoot it out with Peter the Painter, stopping on the way to pick up Winston Churchill. The second chauffeur, Webb, could swear as hard as his master and often did. In Fleet Street he was seen to jump from the driving seat shouting 'You can drive the bloody thing yourself', and Riddell, who had never learned to drive, had to placate his irate driver. But, unlike some others, Webb was never punished for his independence, and both he and his wife were remembered in Riddell's will, together with their child, one of Riddell's many godsons.

Riddell would set off in his car at any hour of the day or night, with Webb at the wheel and Twigg, his valet, beside him. One winter, late in the evening, they began the long trip from Walton Heath to Harrogate and soon the car was slowed by thick fog. Webb, unperturbed by Riddell's sarcasm, told his master that if he stopped blowing snuff in his eyes, he would have a better chance of seeing the road. Somewhere in the Midlands they stopped, completely lost. Webb was commanded to go off and enquire the way while Riddell, buttoned up to the ears in his greatcoat, waited impatiently.

Then Twigg was sent out to search for 'the bloody fool', but on walking round to the back of the car the valet found Webb enjoying a quiet smoke, something that was strictly forbidden when he was driving. 'Don't worry,' whispered the chauffeur, 'I know exactly where we are but I wanted a smoke.' Recounting the story to me nearly twenty years after Riddell's death, Twigg rolled his eyes in mock terror.

On Sunday afternoons Riddell spoke to the Christian Brotherhood, although the members of one such meeting had a shock when they heard their distinguished speaker tell his chauffeur that he was a bloody fool for not being ready at the instant he was required. Why Riddell went to these meetings no one knew. He liked public speaking, even taking elocution lessons to overcome his cockney accent, but he was certainly not a religious man. Even those closest to him never detected that he had any beliefs at all, except in money and power.

'After death,' he said, 'there is nothing but the grave and I don't want a lot of my hard-earned money spent on my funeral. You can dump my body in a bloody ditch as far as I'm concerned.' But he never forgot his early religious training, often saying that he had been brought up on Moody and Sankey. He loved to bring out apt quotations. Of Harry Aldridge who had done well for himself, he said: 'His position today is, of course, mainly due to his own ability and energy but, like the sick at the Pool of Siloam, it is useful to have someone to push you in.'

He once wrote:

To use money requires a special education. I shall have to begin to study philanthropy. One of our professors says the art of true happiness is selfish unselfishness. I think he is right. When Our Lord told the rich young man to give all he had to the poor, he was not thinking of the poor, but of the effect of giving on the young man. There is no doubt that giving oils the wheels of life of the giver.

A millionaire can't take his millions with him when he shuffles off this mortal coil. As the Spaniards say, there are no pockets in shrouds, but if men have no pockets in their shrouds, they have in their trousers, and it's very useful to have something in them.

Money often brings unhappiness. Some men love

74

money for itself. In the old days, when there were no banks and money-lenders stored their money in vaults underneath their houses, they could gloat over their treasures. I wonder whether wealthy people get as much pleasure by looking at their bank books? The satisfactory use of money is a difficult art. The cultured have a great advantage in this respect. They know how to use money to the greatest benefit. They are the patrons of art and literature ...

I rebel against the idea that because you've got money, you're a little god. Of course I know that men are not born equal. Some are cleverer and stronger than others. You can't have quality but you can have a more just division of the products of industry and more consideration of the underdogs by the top dogs ...

At one point he announced to his fellow-directors that he was taking a substantial cut in his salary and that they would have to do the same, while those in retirement after long service would have their pensions reduced. Not only was the economy unnecessary, but Riddell himself had by now accumulated so much wealth that the amount of his annual income was a matter of indifference. Others were not so well placed, but that didn't worry him.

He had always suffered because of uncertainty in his social behaviour, which became apparent especially in his dealings with those under his control. For the aristocracy he had a certain contempt, though he was not reluctant to become acquainted with them. 'You expect the aristocracy,' he said, 'to be completely at their ease because of their position. They're not. In private life they live behind high walls and are rather wary when strangers enter the sacred domain. Every now and then some daring spirit with a witty tongue and endless cheek forces his, or her, way into the charmed circle. The hosts are not at their ease.' Was he thinking of himself?

He was described as one of the best after-dinner speakers

in London. His technique was to arrive late, push on one side the food and drink offered to him, and then deliver an address consisting of a number of stories cleverly strung together. Among the ones suitable to appear in print, are these for lawyers, in the form of verse:

> Here lies the bones of the Brothers Penn,
> Lawyers both, but honest men,
> God works his wonders now and then.

For mixed company: 'The poet says "woman in our hour of ease, uncertain, coy and hard to please".' Riddell would pause, look at the guests over the top of his spectacles, and add: 'Uncertain, yes; coy, perhaps, but judging by their escorts here, certainly not hard to please.'

And for clergymen who had dined well: 'An honest and serious woman, who had heard Dean Inge preach at St Paul's, afterwards asked one of the canons: "Does the Dean believe in Christianity?" "Certainly," replied the canon, "he believes in it, but he doesn't like it very much!"' Riddell also liked to recount how one member of the great Dr Spurgeon's congregation protested when Spurgeon drove to his tabernacle in a gig drawn by two ponies. 'The ponies should not be used on a Sunday,' said this member of the flock. 'Never mind,' said Spurgeon, 'don't worry. Both my ponies were brought up in the Jewish faith.'

Riddell's toughness and unforgiving nature are revealed in his dealings with the printer at the News of the World. 'Why have you been changing the type in my paper?' he demanded. The printer explained the circumstances. 'Bloody fool,' said Riddell who, on this occasion, had reckoned without the spirit of a competent craftsman, who bitingly replied: 'Your blasphemy leaves me cold.' 'Say that again,' thundered Riddell. 'I said your blasphemy leaves me cold.' Riddell never forgave him and cut him out of his will.

There was another scene at the Hotel Cecil (at that time a famous London hotel, now pulled down) when Harry

Aldridge forgot to bring any money to pay for lunch. In those days the price of the set luncheon was 7s. 6d. and a fine meal could be obtained for it, but there was no reduction for those who chose not to take all the courses. Riddell had an egg, a slice of brown bread and a bottle of Vichy water. His companion took all the courses, washed them down with a bottle of stout and then sat back.

'Get the bill,' said Riddell. 'I'm sorry, my Lord, but I've come out without any money.' 'Oh, never mind. Here, waiter, give me the bill.' The waiter brought it to Riddell, who was waiting impatiently to go. It showed two lunches at 15s., plus the cost of the Vichy water and the bottle of stout. Riddell was furious: he hadn't had the full lunch, why 7s. 6d. each? The waiter explained. 'Bloody nonsense,' said Riddell. 'Get the manager. Tell the bloody thief I want to see him.' The manager hurried up and he too explained. 'Well,' said Riddell, 'this is bloody robbery. Do you mean to say that I've been paying 7s. 6d. for years for a bloody egg, a bloody piece of brown bread and a bloody bottle of Vichy water?' 'No, my Lord,' replied the manager. 'Mr Aldridge has always paid.' Riddell never went into the hotel again.

On another occasion Riddell overheard two business men talking about a property they intended to buy, which was going for a song. Riddell quietly slipped out to the telephone. Returning, he tapped one of the men on the shoulder, remarking: 'It's going to cost you more, I'm afraid.' He'd bought it. Telling Aldridge about it he said: 'I didn't pay for lunch that day.' The quick deal greatly amused him.

Emsley Carr scored when Riddell spoke to him about News of the World business while in the Savoy. 'Not so loud,' said Carr, 'See who's over there?' They were rival newspaper owners. 'Don't be silly,' said Riddell, 'they can't hear, they're too far away.' 'Maybe,' replied Carr, 'but perhaps they can lip-read.'

Emsley Carr was not slow in challenging his forceful chairman. Once, when in Carr's view Riddell had criticised the paper unjustly Carr rose from his chair in the editor's room and exploded: 'Either I edit the paper or you do.' Riddell left the room. He knew better than to argue that matter.

# 11 Sentence of Death

In December 1930, Riddell felt ill. He had pains in his back and loins, which were thought to be caused by a chill but, when relief did not come, he entered a London nursing home. He was not an easy patient for his knowledge of medical subjects led him to question his doctors closely about his condition and treatment.

Their task was to convince him that surgery was essential and that the operation would be carried out in two stages. The first would remove the immediate difficulty and was not particularly serious. The second was a major prostate operation which was not without danger.

Riddell considered the situation. He wanted to know the percentage of unsuccessful operations of this kind carried out in London hospitals. The figures were worked out for him and were not favourable, although there were many instances of complete recovery. Then Riddell wanted to know what would happen if he had the first operation but not the second. He got a straight answer: he would live possibly for two years, maybe a little longer, and in acute discomfort.

It was a wretched decision for any man to make, and especially for him. As a solicitor, what would he advise a client in similar circumstances? Success was not guaranteed, and although there was a good chance, it was risky. The alternative was life for at least two years, maybe longer. After twenty-four hours he had made his decision — compromise, the first operation only. To a friend he said: 'I'd rather live like a mouse than die like a lion.' Who will criticise him? Oddly enough, his great friend of the old days, Lloyd George, had to make the same decision, but he didn't hesitate and had both operations. He recovered and lived until he was 82.

After the operation in 1930 Riddell was never the same man: until his death, four years later, he was in constant discomfort; his back was bent and his feet shuffled. Few would blame him for being irritable now.

Lord Rothermere said of him: 'Our admiration for him greatly increased because of the courage — which is the greatest of all virtues — with which he fought illness and attended to his business as if there were really nothing wrong.'

After his convalescence he devoted more time than ever to the affairs of the Royal Free Hospital of which he had become President in 1925. Many were surprised that he had given his support to the Royal Free rather than to St Thomas's, to which Lady Riddell was so greatly attached. The explanation was that St Thomas's were not prepared to make Riddell head of the hospital.

He convinced George Eastman, head of the Kodak Company, that the best site for the Eastman Clinic was next to the Royal Free Hospital, and it was to Riddell that Eastman gave his cheque for £200,000. Jointly with Sir Albert Levy, Riddell responded with an endowment fund of £100,000. Riddell, ever alert to Levy's social aspirations told him that if he would give £50,000 to the clinic, he would introduce him to Queen Mary. This he did at a reception, at which he told Her Majesty the story. The Queen was much amused and shook hands warmly with Sir Albert, whispering to Riddell: 'Are there any more who would like to shake hands with me for £50,000?'

St Thomas's didn't get a penny from him but Lady Riddell saw to it that they did not go short. In her husband's will he had left her £100,000, besides an income of £8,000 a year, and Lady Riddell promptly gave the lump sum to St Thomas's for a nurses' home.

In August 1934 Riddell drove up to the Highland Hotel, Strathpeffer in Inverness-shire. Webb, his chauffeur, Twigg,

Lord Riddell.

The Good Old Days (about 1891).

his valet, and Sister Wright, his nurse, were in the party. In the hotel bedroom he revealed why he had made the journey: he had come to write his will in secret. He sat at a little table in his hotel bedroom, took his old will from his bag and slowly read it through. Then, a sheet at a time, he tore it up and Twigg burnt the pieces in the fireplace, striking a fresh match for each sheet. Riddell watched the paper burn. When all had been reduced to ashes, he told his servant to clean up the grate. He took a fresh paper from his bag, took up his pen and began to write. When his valet went in to see him hours later Riddell was still writing. He did not wish to be disturbed, nor did he want anything.

It was a remarkable will of thirteen foolscap pages, so loosely worded that at least two court decisions were necessary. He had disregarded his own advice that 'Any man who acts as his own lawyer has a fool for a client.' He remembered his newspaper colleagues, his servants, golfing friends, including the caddies, his staff, News of the World men and several charities. The Newspaper Press Fund got a quarter of a million (with much more later) and the Royal Free Hospital the same amount. Churchill received £1,000 as did Lloyd George and Frances Stevenson. There were many others.

Thus he disposed of the fortune he had worked so hard to amass. In January 1935, it was valued at £1,838,901 and re-sworn in 1938 at £2,208,956. What would that be today?

Writing his will had taken a lot out of him. When he returned to Walton Heath he was tired and sick. The journey home from Scotland had been difficult. The party travelled by train and at the various changes, Twigg, Webb and Nurse Wright carried him in a chair to his compartment.

At Walton he recovered sufficiently to walk slowly round the garden, but he frequently needed his local doctor, to whom he said: 'You may think me a damn nuisance, always sending for you, but I will see that you are rewarded in my will.' He forgot.

Nurse Wright was always with him and Lady Riddell came down to stay in the autumn. She had been shocked by her husband's appearance on his return from Scotland. To Dr Binney, Riddell complained: 'Here I am, a millionaire, and nobody can cure me. Is there nothing more that can be done? Is there no new treatment?'

It was a cry from the heart but in vain. The truth was that only the second operation could have saved him and by this time nothing could be done. Riddell feared death and yet he would not carry out the simple instructions given by his doctors. Drinking a lot of water would have given him some relief, but he refused. He looked forward to the visits of Lord Dawson, who came to see him every ten days, and would never agree to any change of treatment unless Dawson approved. 'Are you sure it's all right?' he would ask.

When the weather turned cold he took to his bed in a bare room in the dormy house on the golf course. There he would read and write. There were few visitors, and those who would have liked to have seen him were not encouraged.

In the last stages a little whisky was used to moisten his lips. 'What brand is it?' he whispered. He was told. 'Wrong brand,' he said, 'must have some of Stevenson's.' He meant Lord Stevenson of John Walker's, an acquaintance of World War I. The extraordinary Riddell lay dying, but he had to have the right whisky.

In the last forty-eight hours he refused to see a priest. He sent a telephone message to the paper: 'His Lordship would like to say "goodbye" '. He sent for Twigg: 'Goodbye,' he said, 'and thank you.' He had, according to Twigg, never said thank you before. Gradually he sank into a coma. Nurse Wright attended to his last needs, and on 5 December 1934 he died — a rich, lonely, unhappy man.

Riddell left a letter to his trustees leaving instructions about his newspaper shares, which were worth over one and a half million. They were to be sold to the highest bidder and he wasn't concerned who got them. He named two members of the firm who 'will give the best advice, but possibly with an eye to their own advantage. And why not?'

He instructed that there was to be no mourning and no flowers; and that he was to be cremated and his ashes scattered on Walton Heath Golf Club at the eighth hole, the highest point of the course and furthest from the club house. He asked that there should be no service at St Bride's in Fleet Street but, after a private ceremony at the Brookwood Crematorium, one was held there despite his wishes. The church was crowded, hundreds stood outside, the titled and the famous rubbed shoulders with the humble and unknown. Newspapermen, politicians, doctors, barristers, solicitors, nurses in uniform, heads of hospitals, golfers — all came.

At the last moment, Riddell's old friend, David Lloyd George, walked into St Bride's. The breach was healed.

Lord Beaverbrook paid the finest tribute to Riddell.

Only a man of great attainment could have achieved the results which made his services to the Press so substantial and so honourable. He gave more than his purse; he gave time and care, the dearest gifts of a busy man.

On a winter's evening, when the light had practically gone from the sky, Lady Riddell drove to Walton Heath House. With her she brought a casket. While the shadows lengthened, she walked out on to the golf course with Twigg. She poured out on the grass the ashes of her cousin and husband — George Allardice Riddell. 'That,' she said, 'is the end of him.'

# 12  Fifty Years an Editor

After Riddell's death Emsley Carr succeeded him as Chairman of the News of the World, buying Riddell's shares for a million, raising the money in the City. He was already Editor and, if you judge an editor's success by his paper's circulation as many proprietors do, Emsley Carr was the greatest. Not only the editor who lasted longest, he was the editor who sold most newspapers. When his uncle, Lascelles Carr, gave him the job in 1891, the sales stood at 40,000 copies a week. On his death in 1941 sales were in excess of four million.

He lived a full life, claiming that 'my life is in my newspaper'. While he lived there was not a ripple on the Bouverie Street surface; journalists he took on never left, except to retire or die. His moment of triumph came in 1941 when, at the age of seventy-four, a luncheon was given at the Dorchester to mark his fifty years in the editorial chair. Although it was wartime, Churchill came and spoke, and Beaverbrook attended and Lord Astor, Chairman of The Times, presided. Lord Astor unveiled a portrait of the great Editor, joking 'The Times and the News of the World are not in competition. They publish on different days.'

The King sent a telegram of congratulation and Churchill said: 'When things are not at their best in this country, it is to the journalist people turn for inspiration'. Churchill told how Carr had introduced him to golf — 'a very agreeable and tolerable accompaniment to conversation'. He acclaimed Emsley's record, and then excused himself on the grounds that he must get on with other important affairs. Churchill, himself no mean journalist, contributed to the paper for many years. It was the medium he chose not only

84

for a series called 'The World's Great Stories', but also for 'Great Men' and 'Great Events of our Time'. These were followed by articles forecasting and warning the world of the menace of Hitler. Today, long after Hitler and Mussolini have passed into dark memory, it is fascinating to read in the paper his denunciation of the dictators and of how badly Britain was prepared.

When it celebrated its centenary Churchill sent this message to the News of the World: 'Long may it continue to educate and amuse the British race!' 'Don't forget,' he wrote to the Editor, 'I'm still on the staff and shall expect to be invited to the annual outing.'

Emsley Carr died three months after the celebration luncheon and Percy Davies, his deputy, became Editor.

During the war there was insufficient newsprint to produce all the papers that could be sold, and the number of pages was so restricted that there was only room for the war news, a little sport, some account of the seamy side and a few pin-ups to keep the troops happy. Many of the staff joined the Services and for the first time a woman sub-editor was appointed.

Davies was unassuming, white-haired and usually seen in morning coat and pin-striped trousers. He liked women, whisky and no trouble, and had them all. He once explained the News of the World's reporting technique to me: despite popular belief, he said, the paper did not report all court evidence, which other papers, particularly the Daily Telegraph, printed in full, Girls got into 'a certain condition', they were never pregnant; they were sometimes 'victims of criminal assault', never raped; their clothing was 'disarranged', but never ripped off. Intercourse? Goodness, no! Naked? Certainly not: say unclothed. The paper reported that a man knocked a girl off her bicycle, breaking her nose and bruising her ribs, but 'did not interfere' with her. Later there was allowed a slightly more modern approach; but breasts remained bosoms. A good sub-editor had to know about these things.

The policy of Davies and the other directors was to keep the two cousins — Carr and Jackson — divided. They knew that if ever they got together their own influence would be gone. At first there seemed no cause to fear it happening. The gifted, brave and difficult Derek Jackson (who flew with the RAF and invented a scientific device called 'window', which jammed German radar) wanted no part of the paper, except for the money. The Carrs wanted both. Harry Carr, son of Sir Emsley, had been news editor under Percy Davies before joining the RAF; he was on the board and looked certain to follow as Editor. Also on the board was Derek's representative, Philip (later Sir Philip) Dunn, son of Sir James Dunn, Canadian millionaire and steel tycoon.

Harry Carr started to think about the future. He took some leave and went to see Percy Davies to tell him he would like to be deputy editor and to ask that, if that were not possible because he was in the Air Force, would Davies promise that no one would be appointed until after the war. Harry Carr represented the big Carr interests and had every reason to expect promotion when he came back. But Davies, although appointed Editor and Chairman by Harry's father, wouldn't commit himself. He and the other directors, led by Harry Aldridge and Bertram Jones, could see danger.

Harry Aldridge was a likeable man. Shrewd, bluff, hearty, he was clever at keeping the unions sweet. He'd have the officials in his room, butter them up, pour drinks, enquire about their families and usher them out. Often they forgot what they came for.

He cracked one joke long remembered in Fleet Street. Beaverbrook had invited us both to a surprise party at the Savoy. There was to be entertainment, but the form of it was kept secret. Came the big moment, up went the curtain and there on the platform were a number of little boys, brought all the way from New Brunswick, Canada, to sing carols. There was a pensive look on Aldridge's face and he seemed to be counting. The carols finished. The Express staff stood in respectful silence. Said Beaverbrook to Aldridge: 'Well, what about that?' 'Just like you, Max,' said Harry Aldridge, 'there was one short.' He'd counted the boys and indeed there was one short of a newspaper quire of thirteen. The story went round that another boy was flown from Canada next day.

Bertram Jones aspired to be Chairman. He did become managing director but never got the top post. He came from the business side of the Evening Standard, as Riddell's man. He was a pay-clerk, mean with it and never grew any bigger. His policy was to say 'no', so that he could never be proved wrong. He spent a lot of time learning his part for Masonic occasions, on which he was very keen, and drank most nights in the cellar of the Wellington in Fleet Street. The cellar parties became famous; fortunately drivers did not have to undergo drink tests in those days!

Harry Carr was angry at being rebuffed by Davies, and confided in his twin brother, Walter, known as Wash. They tried to find out who opposed them, but got nowhere. Unhappily, Harry Carr died suddenly and then there was no member of his family on the board. But there were still two sons willing to take on the responsibility; both were in the Services — Walter in the RAF and William (Bill), the youngest, in the Army. Walter had worked on the paper but Bill had started in a small position on the business side before the war. Walter wrote to the board, pointing out that the Carrs were not represented. He can hardly have expected this reply, dated 2 August 1943:

By virtue of a resolution of the board dated 29 December 1941, stating that no additions to the board would be made during the war period unless it was to fill a vacancy caused by the decease or total incapacity of any present active director, it was considered that the present directorate of the board would not be added to in the existing circumstances. It was therefore unanimously resolved that the application of Flight Lieutenant W. C.

Carr that he or his brother, Major W. E. Carr should be invited to join the board of directors of the company could not be favourably considered.

The directors had thrown down the gauntlet and they were to regret it. At this same meeting, which produced that cunning, if wordy minute, another resolution was passed: 'That the board of directors desired to convey to Mrs H. L. Carr and her family their sincere and profound sympathy in the irreparable loss they have so grievously sustained in the passing of Flight Lieutenant H. L. Carr.' Such was the power game inside a great national newspaper.

There followed another reverse for the Carrs. Walter was stricken with the same kidney disease that killed his twin brother. Within months he also was dead. For the Carrs all hopes now rested on the youngest brother, Bill. No one dreamed of the part he was to play.

# 13 Plot at the Coq d'Or

Watching from the wings was Philip Dunn. When it was time for him to make a move, he went to Davies and, astonishingly, was able to convince him that the two positions of chairman and Editor were too much for him. Davies, a weak man faced by a young one representing the great Jackson interests, threw in the towel. What the pressures were are still a mystery. Perhaps Davies didn't want the responsibility of chairmanship anyway, and he certainly could not stomach a running fight between the Jacksons and the Carrs.

Anyway, Dunn convinced him at a meeting over breakfast at Claridge's that it was time for him to step down and, on 8 October 1943, Davies asked the board to relieve him of the chairmanship. He would continue as Editor. His proposal was accepted and Dunn took over. Then Aldridge suggested that the resolution, banning new members of the board for the time being, should be re-affirmed. That was passed too, plus another resolution that, when the board thought it desirable to fill any vacancies, they would favourably consider senior executives.

So a Jackson man was now in the chair; the Carrs, the biggest shareholders, were out, and there was a minute that would stop them coming back, or so it was thought. Bill Carr bided his time. 'Let's get the war over first,' he said. Besides, he had another problem: with the deaths of his father, his mother and two brothers within a short period, an enormous sum was needed to meet death duties.

Dunn, still in the Army, was anxious to get out and on with the job. Brendan Bracken, then Minister of Information, told Jones that the paper should write saying that Dunn was of greater service to the nation running the News of the World than he was taking newspaper correspondents round the Front. 'I told Bracken,' said Jones, 'that I did not feel such a letter would be justified. Besides, what about our other men in the Services? All should be treated alike.' A Ministry of Labour official then made an approach and said he understood that Jones had been in touch with the Ministry of Information requesting a specially early release for Captain Dunn, to which Jones retorted: 'We are getting on very nicely without him, thank you.' When Dunn was released, he and Jones never seemed to hit it off.

Philip Dunn, then a slim young man with a hesitant manner, set himself up in a magnificent suite on the fourth floor of 30 Bouverie Street. He hadn't a clue about running a newspaper, but he got a man who did — Robert Skelton from the Daily Telegraph, a deputy who would breathe down the Editor's neck. The technique is not unknown in Fleet Street. Dunn saw the paper as a political power, with himself pulling the levers. He brought in new blood, increased salaries and encouraged Skelton to appoint correspondents in New York, Paris, Rome and other world capitals. It was the first time the paper had a foreign department. The expenses rose but so did the circulation.

Skelton ran the paper on Daily Telegraph lines. 'News, more news,' he said, 'give the foreign correspondents more space.' He held that with the troops coming home they would be interested in countries they had served in, besides their own, and their minds would have broadened. They would also, Skelton thought, want to know about jobs, housing and sport, and take an interest in politics and what they had been fighting for. They would also want to know more about social security and the health service. He was right and by getting top writers on these subjects, the paper captured even more readers. The circulation rose to an all-time high of eight and a half million.

The directors didn't understand this widening of

horizons. But what could they do? After their treatment of his family they could scarcely invite Carr to come to their rescue and fight Dunn. In the event they didn't need to do anything. Carr fired the first shot in what was to be a lengthy battle. From his Army station in Europe, he wrote to say that the Carrs were still the biggest shareholders and he would like to join the board.

Dunn replied: 'Thank you very much, but I don't want you on the board and neither do any of the other directors.' That was debatable: the other directors were getting fed up with Dunn, and were highly critical of the financial and political ways in which he ran the company.

Dunn and Skelton backed Churchill to the hilt and beyond in the 1945 election, while Winston himself wrote on the leader page. The front page splashed his 'Tour of Triumph' and the opinion column proclaimed: 'This man must lead us in peace as in war.' There was not a word about Labour supporters who, when the vote was taken, put Churchill out and Attlee in. The paper had not been too clever in backing the wrong one in a two-horse race — years later it did it again — and there were as many Labour readers as Tory, probably more.

The directors decided that the political issue was the one on which to fight Dunn. It was discussed at a board meeting and Dunn insisted that he had a right to instruct the leader writers on political policy. The other directors didn't agree. The Articles of Association made it clear that the Editor was appointed by the board and that the managing director was responsible for the day-to-day running of the paper. The chairman should not interfere. There was a furious row but, at that stage, nothing came of it, for the directors knew they couldn't get Dunn out while Jackson backed him. Not yet anyway.

At that time Carr went to live at Halland in Sussex and to think over how he might extend his influence and get on to the board. First he had to decide whether he would fight Dunn. He talked it over with Jean, his wife. 'Shall we fight?'

asked Bill. 'We can get out with enough to live on, about £200,000. But I shall lose my way of life.' 'Fight!' counselled his wife. 'I shouldn't have done so' Bill Carr said, 'if Jean hadn't persuaded me.'

Bill Carr had what we called an inspiration. With his solicitor, John Brooks, and helped by a mutual friend, the Earl of Warwick, he made contact with Derek Jackson, who was then living in Ireland. Could they co-operate? Derek would not do so at first but he gradually became more amiable and Warwick helped things along. The Warwicks knew how to play king-makers. Carr next drafted a letter pledging all his family's voting shares to Dunn, so that Dunn would remain Chairman for life.

Carr had no intention of signing this pledge, but he wondered how the other directors would react to it, and, as he had judged, they were alarmed. He told them that if they did not elect him to the board he would support Dunn as Chairman and keep him there. More than that, if they did not do as he wished, when he had made Dunn secure for life, Dunn would make him a director out of gratitude, and the two of them would make it hot for the others. 'They didn't care for that at all,' said Carr. 'They held a board meeting within a week and I was elected.'

Carr's family finances were still in a tangle. He and his sisters were not even getting an income because of death duties, and they had no representation on the board of their newspaper, which constituted the whole of the family fortune. All other liquid assets, even the shares that they had held for many years in the Western Mail of Cardiff, had been disposed of. Something had to be done. Brooks undertook to see that the income situation was sorted out immediately.

News of the World ordinary shares were held under limited articles and were subject to restriction on transfer. In broad terms, the Jackson family, through trustees, held nearly one-third of the shares; the Carrs, through their trustees, held a little more than one-third; and the general public, most of them former employees or people who had helped the firm in its early days of struggle, held the remaining one-third. When the company went public in 1959, the shares remained in the same proportions. That was a critical factor in the battle to come.

Carr's next thought was how to unseat Dunn and become Chairman in his place. On 30 October 1947 the directors lunched at the Coq d'Or off Piccadilly. Dunn left early and, when he'd gone, Carr remarked that the other directors didn't seem to be getting on well with their Chairman. Why didn't they get rid of him, which they could do simply by voting him off? If Dunn, acting for the Jacksons, called for a poll by which the shareholder commanding the biggest backing would win, he felt that the Carrs and their supporters would beat the Jacksons.

Carr got the directors to agree to put it to the test. They didn't much care for Carr but they hated Dunn and besides, Carr was being agreeable. He suggested that Aldridge should become Chairman, Jones, managing director, and he, Carr, vice-chairman. Aldridge, who was close to retirement, was acceptable to the others, and Carr did not wish to appear hungry for power, even if he were.

Little did Dunn realise when he left the Coq d'Or that day that those who remained at the luncheon had 'fixed' him. They returned to the office to compose a letter telling him that they didn't want him any more. Aldridge got it typed, each director signed it and they sent it to Dunn's office. Dunn was outraged. He hurried to·Bouverie Street early on the morning of 4 November 1947 to tell the board that if they wouldn't have him as Chairman, he would stay on as an ordinary director. Carr did not oppose this, so Dunn got out of the chair, congratulated Aldridge on taking over and sat down on the other side of the table. Then Jones spoke. The situation was impossible, he said. Dunn would no longer be permitted to give orders to the Editor or hold editorial conferences; nor as an ordinary director, would he be able to occupy his suite of offices on the fourth floor. In addition, the other directors were 'fed-up' with him.

Dunn declared that Jackson would not agree to his being kicked out altogether, and Jones countered that the board would welcome Jackson himself, or another representative, but not Dunn. Jones smelled blood and pressed his advantage. Then Aldridge clinched it from the chair. In blunt terms, he told Dunn that they were all against him. He hadn't a friend left; it was in the paper's best interests that he should go. The board were ready to discuss terms.

Dunn realised that he was beaten and took £50,000 free of tax to soothe his feelings. To his Editor, Bob Skelton, the board voted £20,000, also free of tax, in return for his resignation. He was a Dunn man and that was sufficient reason. Besides, Skelton would never take orders from the directors. He didn't ask them how to edit the paper. In his view, Editors carried out the board's policy, but exactly how was the Editor's business. Beyond keeping to the policy, Skelton would brook no interference. That was the News of the World tradition: it was one for which I fought in 1970 — and for which I got sacked.

# 14 When it was Fun

Before the war I was with the Daily Telegraph and the News Chronicle, and was highly respectable and badly paid. I joined the News of the World in 1945, having just been demobbed from the army. Because I was a Territorial who had gone in at the beginning and had reached the ripe old age of 34, I was among the early ones to change from khaki into a demob suit of unspeakable colour and cut. I got a new suit with my first pay cheque. When I went to the News of the World I wasn't badly paid.

But that didn't happen until after the war was over. In 1938 some of us who were working on newspapers and in the theatre got fed up with Hitler's threats and joined the 2nd Battalion Queen's Westminsters. We were able to drill two mornings a week at Buckingham Gate as we worked at nights, as did the actors. What an odd mob we were, drawn from Fleet Street and the theatres of the West End. Even the British Army couldn't stand that, so we were split up, sent to Officer Cadet Training Units and commissioned in various regiments. I went to the Gloucesters.

The day I came out of the army at the end of the war, and still in uniform, I walked into the News Chronicle office and asked to see the Editor, Gerald Barry. He didn't remember the young man who had joined the editoral staff six years earlier for the princely sum of £10 a week, which was eleven shillings more than I got at the Telegraph. He said I could have my old job back. But I said I wanted the promotion that would have fallen to me had I not gone off to the war. He was not impressed.

'I didn't expect you to put down a red carpet,' I said. 'I didn't do anything disgraceful — just joined the army.'

Perhaps I shouldn't have got cross and told him what I thought of the liberal News Chronicle. But I did and slammed out.

It is only fair to add that my colleagues were angry too. They had seen to it that I got an allowance for my family of £5 a week while I was in the Services.

So, in the army one moment, out of work the next. I walked up White Friar Street, turned into Fleet Street and into the bar of the Punch. I had never been there before and what a stroke of luck it was that I needed a drink.

Standing at the end of the bar was a military-looking figure that was well known to me. It was Bob Skelton, night editor of the Daily Telegraph when I worked there. He asked me what I was doing and when I said that I had just walked out of the News Chronicle, he told me that he had just been made deputy-editor of the News of the World. Could I join him tomorrow? 'Yes' I said. We drank to it and parted. That was quick, I thought. What job am I going to get and what about pay? Had I been rash? Anyway, I'd only been out of work five minutes.

There was no need to worry; Skelton was good to me and gave me many exciting stories to cover, and it wasn't long before I was writing the leading article. Skelton always told me the score. But soon a crisis loomed and, looking back, it does seem that trouble followed me around.

Skelton and I were drinking champagne one Saturday morning in El Vinos — *the* Fleet Street bar. It was cheaper then. I'd written the leader, but every Saturday at noon I had to read it over the telephone to the Chairman, Philip Dunn, no matter where he was. (At this stage Dunn was still in charge.)

'Time for me to read the leader to the boss,' I said. 'To hell with the boss, I'm the Editor,' said Skelton, which he was. I didn't read the leader to the boss; I went on drinking champagne. On Tuesday morning I was sent for: 'You didn't read the leader to me on Saturday morning,' said Dunn. 'Why?' What could I say? I couldn't repeat my

The Blitz, World War II. The offices were knocked about but the paper was never stopped.

My Office. The famous editor's chair in the foreground and Sir Emsley,
editor for 50 years, on the wall.

Taking a look at one of our horses with Sir Gordon Richards.

On the telly, with Editors Gunn, Valdar, Hetherington, Hardcastle, Howard and Somerfield. Lord Birkett is in the chair.

conversation with Skelton. I could only apologise. 'That's the last time you'll write a leader in this paper,' said Dunn. He was right but only for the moment.

I didn't blame him for taking the tough line; on the face of it I deserved to be sacked. But I had not shopped Skelton and he stood by me; something Editors don't always do. He kept me out of Dunn's way, sent me to the Peace Conference in Paris and gave me many other worthwhile assignments. I was happy. Skelton made me Foreign Editor, and I shall not forget the day our man in the Middle East, Richard Wyndham, got a sniper's bullet in his head. Wyndham wasn't the sort of man the News of the World old-timers were used to. They had a fit when he bought an aeroplane on the paper and put in a gigantic expense sheet when he crashed it. Dick liked driving open motor cars, his hair streaming in the wind and a beautiful blonde by his side. A most talented man who had wretched luck. A reporter's job can be a dangerous one.

I didn't find the Paris Conference dull. Our man there, a bearded reporter from the Telegraph with a delicious sense of humour, fixed me up with a French 'secretary-bird' who read the papers to me in bed in the mornings, which was most necessary as my French was very poor. She not only read the papers; she looked after my clothes, she knew exactly what tips to leave and where the best food was to be found. In a time of rationing that was most satisfactory. I didn't go short of anything. Sadly we parted; I paid her modest bill and never heard of her again. Rather a pity!

I flew out to Malta to meet the crew of the *Amethyst*, the courageous British destroyer that defied the Communist guns, escaped down the Yangtse River and rejoined the Fleet. Commander Kerrens, with the Nelson touch, signalled in triumph 'God Save the King!' It was a thrilling story and gave the nation a lift at a bad time. My hope was to invite the crew to London to have dinner, but how to fix it? Fortunately for me — and reporters need luck — I met a sailor friend who happened to be on the C-in-C's staff.

97

'I'll get you in to see the C-in-C,' he said; and he did. It was Admiral Power, a very tough cookie indeed. He was a brawny chap, tall and tough, with tattooed arms. He kept me standing while he lectured for ten minutes on the evils of the Press. It was a hot day and I got a bit bored with this. I stopped him in full flight: 'Sir, you have lectured me on the evils of the Press. I now propose to speak about the evils of the Royal Navy.' I was ready with Churchill's famous quip: vice, lice, buggery and the lash. But there was no need. The Admiral gave a great laugh at my impertinence: 'Come to lunch,' he said. I was in.

The party at the Dorchester was a 'wow'. The First Sea Lord, Admiral Fraser of North Cape, came, gave the V-sign and kissed the Windmill girls. The sailors loved it. The girls were always my favourites. Their fee was a pair of silk stockings each — so much more attractive than tights, which, thankfully, were not available then. Silk stockings took a lot of finding in those days of shortages, but we managed it. The star of the show was Jack Benny and his fee was a large cigar. And they say he was mean!

On another occasion we invited all holders of the VC to dinner and brought them to London. VCs come from all walks of life and few had been to the Dorchester before. Some brought their families, which I hadn't bargained for. We scrapped the table plan and the menu, and said to the hotel staff: 'These chaps are heroes; give them anything they ask for; champagne and caviar or fish and chips, it doesn't matter.' Some preferred fish and chips and a pint; some, several pints!

We took the whole of an hotel in Kensington for them to stay in. I'd never gone into an hotel before and said: 'I'll take all your rooms. Yes, that's right, the lot.' Then the VCs didn't want to go home. They kept on asking Piper Laidlow to play the pipes once more; and he played as he did on the parapet at Loos in World War I, and the VCs charged over the tables as the troops had charged in Flanders.

The police 'played ball' that night. I telephoned and said

we had some VCs at a party and there might be a bit of a problem getting them home. They understood and sent squad cars to assist, not to arrest.

Joan, my wonderful secretary who was with me until I left the paper, sorted out our heroes. Not all got into the right bedrooms and one lost his false teeth down the lavatory. Joan got him another set.

The next difficulty was to persuade our guests that they had to return to their homes at some time. Joan put the last one on a train after about a week. It was all great fun, but there were also some tears. The widow of Guy Gibson, leader of the Dam Busters, arrived at the Dorchester unexpectedly. She was crying bitterly and all I could do was to fill her arms with flowers.

I was keen to go to a horse race in France and, with little time to spare, borrowed a plane from Vivian Van Dam, the boss of the Windmill. 'Meet my pilot under the clock at Victoria,' he said. With Phil Ashmore, our great little racing man, I stood under the clock at the appointed time. There was nobody about save for a beautiful blonde with the most penetrating blue eyes. Could she be the pilot? She was, and only the fear of appearing afraid caused Phil and me to go through with the trip. But she flew the plane beautifully and, on landing in France, we borrowed a battered Citroën and drove to the course with about ten others hanging on. It was quite a day.

With Ronnie Collier of the Daily Mail I sailed with the Navy to the West Indies, and got into bad odour with Lord Hall, the First Lord, who was also making the trip. He threatened to censor my message, which was highly critical of him. 'Do that,' I said, 'and my next message will say "First Lord censors News of the World story in peacetime".' He thought better of it. His Lordship embarrassed the sailors by severely criticising the Press, but Collier, a lively wit, told the story of the three little boys who said their names were Aneurin, Clement and Herbert — distinguished politicians of their day. Their schoolteacher wrote to their mother. 'Dear Mrs Smith,' she said, 'can this be true?' 'I'm not Mrs Smith,' came the answer. 'I'm Miss Smith; can you think of better names for the three little bastards?' The sailors roared.

We were taken round the flagship on a dignified tour. I found myself the last of the line. Suddenly a heavy tattooed arm shot out from the heads (lavatories) and a voice growled in my ear: 'Don't believe a bloody word of it, mate, the food's terrible.' I wrote that, and got a message from the ship that there had been a marked improvement.

I got to the flagship by crossing to her from a destroyer while both ships were moving at speed. It was done by something called a jackstay and I was terrified. I expected to slip from the loop and to be dashed into the sea and cut to pieces by the screws of the two ships. But all went well and I landed trembling on the flagship to be greeted by Wee McGregor, the Admiral himself. 'I suppose you do this every day,' I said. 'Good God no,' he replied. 'I wouldn't do it.' I refused the return trip by jackstay: the ships stopped for me and I was rowed back in due form.

All in all, the newspaper life could be exciting. We flew from the West Indies by hitching a lift in a plane — one could do that in those days — and landed, without money, in New York. I expected to be thrown out, but no, the immigration officer knew all about the News of the World. He was Irish. 'My mother posts it to me every week,' he said. 'Stay as long as you like.'

Earlier, on the Dutch island of Curaçao, we had spent the night in gaol because my jolly friend, asked to state what arms we carried, wrote down: ten machine-guns, six revolvers, twelve hand grenades and a tank. They put us inside for being funny. The guardhouse was white-washed and spotlessly clean. Next day we were shoved on a plane which put down in the Bahamas. What should we do while awaiting funds from England? We discussed the point in a restaurant while considering doing the washing up as payment for our dinner. We hadn't a dime between us.

Our luck held. We were overheard by a lady sitting at the next table. She took pity on us, paid our bill, gave us a bed for the night and lent us $500. 'When you get to New York,' she said, 'ring this number. It's my solicitor, and when you get your money from London, pay him.' What trust! From Grand Central Station, as instructed, we telephoned, met the lawyer and handed back the $500. 'I told my client she was crazy,' he said. 'I told her: You'll never see your money again.' He was so surprised and pleased that he took us out for a splendid dinner.

Eventually we got back to London, via Washington, Gander and Iceland and, as you might expect, nobody was the slightest bit interested. There were other reporters besides us, and nothing is as old as yesterday's news.

# 15 When it was Sad

The day that Robert Skelton was fired from the editorship was a bad one for me. I'd been waiting in my room wondering what was going on upstairs. Dunn came in first, shook hands and said good luck and goodbye. He was off, he said, and so was Skelton. Arthur Waters was the new Editor. Dunn noticed my gloom and said he hoped I wouldn't get the bullet, which was nice. My next visitor was Waters, who rushed in, and, without a word, pulled Dunn's picture off the wall and smashed it in the fireplace. He went out, which was just as well, as I had started to laugh.

Skelton was the next to arrive. He was beaming and holding up a cheque. It was for £20,000, which was real money in those days. 'What shall we do with it?' he said. 'Spend it,' I suggested. So we collected Joyce, his secretary, and one or two others, and took a taxi to the Royal Automobile Club where we proceeded to drink champagne until it was closing time or there wasn't any left; one or the other. 'We haven't spent all the cheque,' I said, 'but we've made a dent in it.'

We got a bed somewhere and next morning I returned to the office. Joyce met me in tears, saying that Waters had locked her out of her room. I found a key and she collected her belongings and left. I sat at my desk, awaiting the summons. It had to come, and it did. 'Where have you been?' Waters demanded, beads of sweat on his long, sallow face. I noticed he was wearing a new suit, the first for years. 'I've been out with the Editor,' I said, with innocence, I hoped, gleaming from my blood-shot eyes. 'I'm the Editor now,' he said. 'Oh my God,' was all I could manage. 'You will see Mr Aldridge, the new Chairman, at three o'clock', said Waters gleefully. 'He is going to fire you.' 'That's all for the best,' I said.

Gloomily I took lunch alone, going over in my mind what I would say to Aldridge. Ought I to suffer because Waters didn't like me and because I was a friend of Skelton? We were friends before we ever came to the News of the World. It seemed a bit rough. I was pretty miserable and my head didn't help much either.

At five to three I walked up to Aldridge's little office on the second floor 'no ornate room with a giant desk like Dunn's for him'. But I never reached it. As I passed Bill Carr's room he came out. He had been waiting. 'Do you want to go?' he asked. 'No,' I said. 'Then don't go,' said Bill. 'Waters won't be here for ever.'

We shook hands; Bill knew how I was feeling. I retraced my steps down the corridor, mounted the stairs to the third floor. Waters was waiting: 'Well?' he queried. 'Don't get your bowels in an uproar,' I said. 'I'm staying.' And I did — for twenty more years.

Aldridge had a peaceful chairmanship, with Carr as his deputy and Bertram Jones as managing director. I suffered under Arthur Waters, one of the old Welsh School, who had been on the paper for many years. He could write like Charles Dickens — well almost — perhaps on an off-day. He didn't let the facts interfere with a good story. When we couldn't find a picture of the famous white horse at the Wembley Cup Final — the horse with the policeman on its back who controlled the crowds when they surged on to the pitch — he had one painted in. He would read the agency news, throw it away and write something better. He loved seamy court stories, his wife Maudie and putting a shilling on a horse. Maudie owned a horse called Young Sport. Maudie herself was a jolly good sport and owned a pub in Covent Garden. Waters would leave the office at ten on a Saturday night, no matter what news was coming in. His more important job was to count the money in the till at the pub, see the barmaids had nothing belonging to the house concealed in their bloomers and pour all slops of beer left in the glasses back into the barrel.

As soon as he became Editor, his first task, he said, was to save the firm's money. He vowed he would get back in a year the sum that Dunn and Skelton had collected; and he did. He sacked all foreign correspondents, pruned the staff, refused to buy anything and stopped the daily papers.

We never seemed to meet. He never lunched out unless it was free; drank out of a large white mug with his name on it in scarlet letters; went home at three, or thereabouts, after the big race. He had a long, lugubrious face and the largest bags under his eyes I have ever seen. He never drank anything but tea. Tea-drinking is a great habit in newspaper offices. Sub-editors think nothing of drinking twenty cups or more in a night. I know, I've done it many times! Waters would cut his long finger nails with a large pair of scissors, and we had to cover our cups with our hands so that the pieces didn't fly in.

'Come in,' he would say, 'my door is always open.' And he believed it. I saw him in tears one day when he sacked a reporter, but he put the knife in just the same; and twisted it. He was indifferent to criticism, and watched the circulation stand still and then fall; but he knew how to look after himself. The chairman once asked him to whom he owed loyalty. It was a silly question. 'To Arthur G. Waters,' was the instant reply. His editorship came in a difficult time. The war was over and families were together again. There wasn't so much duplication of sales; television was starting up and newspapers didn't yet know how to compete with it. It was a time of depression and rationing.

Waters ploughed on as if nothing was happening, and he didn't give a hoot about what our rivals were doing, which, in other circumstances, might have been a good thing.

I once got excited and said: 'The Sunday Express has a great story in its first edition.' Replied Waters: 'Is that so, I must remember to get a copy tomorrow.' It didn't enter his head that we might make our own enquiries and pick up the story for later editions. He also stopped my daily papers, saying they were unnecessary.

He became rich, mostly because he never spent a penny. After Maudie died, which hurt him a great deal, he lived in a little two-up, two-down cottage, and never went anywhere.

But he could write dramatically, which suited a popular paper of that day: 'the corn was well cooked.' Consider this:

> The black cap is adjusted on the head of Mr Justice Talbot, the law is spoken in a court hushed and reverent, and with the words 'may the Lord have mercy on your soul', Rouse turns and goes with rapid strides from view. From the public seats comes the cry 'Oh, Arthur, Arthur:' It is the end.

And this:

> Behind the suicide in a South Kensington flat of a handsome woman in her twenty-fifth year, lies the story of a country girl caught in the butterfly life of London and drawn to a wretched death.

And this:

> He conducted an affair with two wives, one married bigamously, and two other ladies, all on £8 a week, living a life which, as history tells us, has ruined empires, toppled thrones, and brought millionaires to poverty and disgrace.

£8 a week must have gone a long way then.

Waters had been the theatre critic at one time, and had a huge stock of Scotch and cigars, collected from actors and managers grateful for complimentary notices. These he sold. He read only one daily paper — the News Chronicle —

unless he was able to pick up another in the train on the way to work, from Horley in Surrey.

He announced the end of the war on the wrong day, but that didn't worry him unduly, even though the edition was called back. He once rewrote my report about a fishing boat lost at sea. He described the sorrow of the bereaved families, and told vividly how he 'walked the rain-soaked streets of the little town of tears', pausing to listen outside dimly lighted windows. From within he could hear the sound of 'For those in peril on the sea'. But he got the name of the town wrong!

Arthur Waters was the Editor who complimented a young reporter on his brilliant story about a mine disaster. He had beaten the top men of Fleet Street. 'Let me see now, how much are you getting?' asked Waters. 'Four pounds a week, Sir,' replied the lad. 'Oh I *am* glad,' said Waters. (Some declare this happened in Cardiff, but News of the World men will always maintain that Waters was the Editor concerned. He had to be; the story fits him so perfectly.)

Waters believed that what sold papers was sex, crime, beer and cricket in the summer; football in winter. So did I, but not only that. I also believed that, after the war, men and women in a new age wanted more. In Britain there were six and three-quarter million young marrieds in the twenty to thirty-four age group, who spent most of their time at home, as their children were young. They were interested in housing, the health service, education and employment.

We had established the John Hilton Bureau to sort out their problems, employing a staff of a hundred experts to deal with thousands of letters a week. We also looked after the problems of the elderly, and if there was unfairness or red tape, we did something about it.

Officials and ministries were usually ready to assist. They had to be, for they knew we would 'clobber' them if necessary. We also realised that the chief leisure activities of this group were watching television, reading and gardening, 'do-it-yourself' jobs about the house, listening to the radio and knitting. A newspaper editor has to be aware of these and other statistics. In the thirty-five to forty-four age group many women go back to work after family responsibilities are reduced. Even then, 40 per cent had a motor car, many more today. Then there were thirteen million people in the forty-five to sixty-four group, of whom a high percentage was chiefly interested in home ownership, a car and holidays abroad.

Two other groups were important: the teenagers with money to spend, whose interests were sex, clothes, dancing and records; and finally the elderly, who had more time for reading and watching television. Nor could one overlook the millions on pensions and supplementary allowances. A newspaper must provide for all those groups and try to get the proportions right. There is more to it than sex, sport, beer and football, though to forget these would be fatal. Waters overlooked Riddell's doctrine that a newspaper should provide news of the people for all the people, and Emsley Carr's words: 'The News of the World is a human document representing the daily life of the average man — not neglecting the more serious problems, but also touching on the lighter forms of life, bringing humour, brightness and humanity into everyone's existence.'

Waters would read proofs after we'd gone to press and put the wind up John Hinchcliffe, our legal man, by saying, 'My God, don't tell me you've passed that.' It was a bit nerve-racking for him, but he was rarely at fault, if ever.

Waters fought a running battle with Norman Rae, our top crime reporter, who was just as great a character as Waters himself. 'Come in, Norman, you are going to tell me that Setty's head has been found in the estuary of the Thames,' he said sardonically one day. It was a remarkable guess. For that's just where Setty's head was found, thrown from a plane.

Norman had him beaten, though, over another murder, this time in Wales. Waters swore Rae would be scooped by rival crime men, and Norman worked hard to prevent it and to prove to Waters who was the best crime-reporter in Fleet Street. He got the story first and phoned Waters to tell him, but, to his dismay and annoyance, the Editor had gone home that Saturday night and died. Rae was most upset that he never heard about the scoop: nobody else was.

Top detectives were known to hold up Press conferences until Norman arrived. I once went with him to his home town of Aberdeen, on a story about a boy who had stolen a yacht and taken it to sea single-handed. A nice little adventure story, but we were somewhat hampered by the possibility of a criminal charge. Waters quite rightly warned us on the phone about the danger of contempt of court. 'Not to worry, Mr Waters,' said Norman, 'The boy won't be charged until after we've gone to press.' 'How do you know?' asked Waters, 'How can you be sure?' 'Well, ask the Chief Constable, he's right here.' and the Chief Constable replied: 'That's quite right Mr Waters, if Norman says so.'

Reginald Cudlipp, one of the three famous Cudlipp brothers, took over from Waters. It was an extraordinary achievement that each of the Cudlipps — Percy, Reg and Hugh — were all Fleet Street editors at the same time. Hugh, now a peer, went on from one success to another in the newspaper field.

Reg had a tough time. Waters had not left a buoyant paper and the staff were not happy. I was given the post of Northern Editor, and fought to free the Manchester editions from London's restrictive grasp. Cudlipp was a master of detail and he was happiest when doing everything himself, which he did with great skill, working longer hours than anyone. But you can't produce a modern newspaper like that; the Editor must delegate.

The circulation kept falling, which was heart-breaking for the Editor, who worked even longer hours, slashing articles, rewriting, putting on new headlines, making up the paper, writing leaders. But all to no avail. He thought that television was causing sales to fall and that people no longer spent a lot of time reading at the weekend: if they weren't gazing at the box they were out in their motor-cars.

After two years in Manchester I was appointed deputy-editor and returned to London. Clearly no one was happy. The next person to go was Aldridge on reaching the age of seventy; then Jones retired and Cudlipp was paid off. At long last Bill Carr became Chairman, a move that changed my life.

# 16 In the Hot Seat

Bill Carr sent for me. He was sitting in his West End flat suffering, as he often did, from gout. I've seen sweat run down his face from the pain, but he never complained, did not ask for sympathy and didn't encourage one to offer it. 'What the hell kept you,' he said. What had kept me was helping Cudlipp clear out his desk. He was a meticulous man and, among other things, he carefully handed me the petty cash of £50, counting it twice, just to make sure. He ruefully pointed to a splendid pair of cufflinks. 'They only gave me those at Christmas,' he said. I opened the lift-gates for him, said goodnight and watched him leave. One thing he could have been pleased about: in those days the Inland Revenue took a more relaxed view of severance pay.

Carr told me to pour a drink, adding: 'I wanted you to be Editor before this, but there were difficulties.' I knew what he meant.

Not all the directors thought that I was the man for the job, particularly Jones, the managing director, who, I thought, was a wet and said so. He eventually left, rich, still saying 'no' and full of masonic ritual. 'I have spoken to Derek (Jackson),' said Carr, 'and he supports you, so I am offering you the job.'

I had waited for this moment (not always patiently) for many years. I wanted to get my hands on the paper before the downward slide became so fast that no one could stop it. I knew that if I failed I would get the reward of all failed editors — the bullet and no messing about. But I knew that the staff, with a couple of exceptions, would back me, that the Chairman was behind me, and I knew what I wanted to do. This was my life. 'Thank you, I said. 'I'll take a chance.'

On my first day in the Editor's chair I called the staff together, pushed out the boat and said: 'What the hell are we going to do about the circulation? It's going down the drain. It's still the largest, but won't continue so if we go on like this. We want a series of articles that will make their hair curl. We haven't had one for years.'

We came up with the life story of Diana Dors, the ash-blonde who had led a not altogether sheltered life; films and fun, in that order. She made the sales soar and my backside sore from the kicks I received from those who thought her memoirs highly improper. But we were talked about, and that's what I wanted.

I also knew that we must change our style and brighten the make-up. It was the day of investigative journalism, the story behind the story. It was not enough to print straightforward court reports, though these had to be retained. I thought that we might relax the rules a bit and use a little more up-to-date language, as long as it was straightforward, sharp and simple. We also needed to brighten up the pages, use bigger pictures and bigger type. But, and of that I was sure, we shouldn't do too much too soon. The paper must be recognisable to all our old readers while we gained new ones. I urged the staff to be bolder, but not careless, and, in fact, to improve all round. The Northern Editor was to be given a freer hand with his Scottish, Irish and north-country editions. Above all, we had got to be talked about. That last was not difficult to achieve.

Bernard Levin let fly at me on television: he accused me of unwholesomely exploiting sex, evading the truth, not only giving the public what they wanted, but creating the demand as well as satisfying it. That was going it a bit — especially when he threw in that we were self-righteous. I enjoyed his performance, although I thought he overplayed it. I had to remind him that to get our paper, people had to go out and buy it, or arrange for it to be delivered. It was not thrust on them, like television. It was a matter of choice and he, obviously, had chosen to read it closely.

Actually, Miss Dors's story was as mild as ass's milk compared with much that is published and shown on the screens today. It was her life and it was frankly told. I saw no reason to change or censor it. The paper was published for adult people. We got pretty heated about it in the end.

The Press Council got shirty too, but we pressed on with the story, sending relays of reporters down to the Dors's home at Maidenhead to extract the last ounce of material. She gave it and they enjoyed getting it. More television appearances followed. Jeremy Thorpe, an old friend and MP for Barnstaple, Devon, where I was born, was tough.

I was a member of a panel called 'The Editors,' composed of Herbert Gunn (Sunday Dispatch), William Hardcastle (Daily Mail), Alastair Hetherington (Guardian), Lee Howard (Sunday Pictorial) and Colin Valdar (Daily Sketch). Lord Birkett was in the chair, and we were questioned by three MPs, Sir John Foster QC (Conservative), Judith Hart (Labour) and Jeremy Thorpe (Liberal): a formidable lot.

Lord Birkett kicked off by asking me what I thought the real purpose of a newspaper was. A tough one to reply to in a paragraph, as we were asked, and put by one of the best cross-examiners of his day. I replied: 'I rely on the words of Winston Churchill, who said of the News of the World: "Long may it continue to educate and amuse the British race." I don't think I can improve on that.' Then Jeremy weighed in. He didn't spare an old Liberal like myself. This is how the exchange went:

*Thorpe* Do you agree with the stricture of the Press Council that the conduct of your paper in regard to the Diana Dors articles allowed standards to be debased and, I quote, to a level which was a disgrace to British journalism? Would you say that was part of your job of useful instruction or of valuable adult amusement?
*Somerfield* The Press Council were quite out of step in saying that. They were trying to exercise control on the

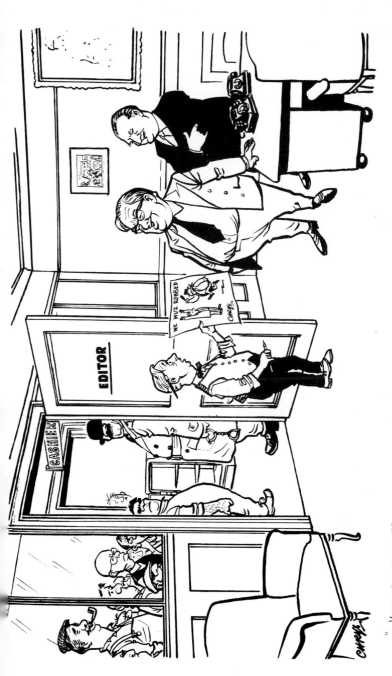

The day the safe was robbed. Carr in dark suit, Lear with pipe, and Stanley Strong the bald-headed printer.

Editor, 1960, making a broadcast.

contents of a newspaper. That's not their job at all. Their task should be to control behaviour. This is something they have lost sight of. Of course I don't agree with what they say. The Diana Dors story was fascinating; instead of the usual six and a half million people buying the paper, many thousands more read it. Who is to say they were wrong?

*Thorpe* Let me get down to some phrases. 'As I hit the floor my dressing-gown burst open revealing my naked body to our guests'. Now what sort of principle of journalism do you feel you are enhancing by printing that sort of thing. Would you say that this was one of the more important contributions of which you are particularly proud as a journalist?

*Somerfield* I am proud of the paper as a whole.

*Thorpe* Could you answer the question?

*Somerfield* I'm not in the witness box, Mr Thorpe.

*Thorpe* Would you say that that particular series of articles is something of which you are particularly proud as a journalist, or the reverse?

*Somerfield* I shall answer in my own way. I am saying that I am proud of the paper, and this was a part of it; I thought an extremely interesting part, but only a part.

*Thorpe* I want to ask you about news. If you look at your issue of 17 July 1960, on the front page is a murder story, which I concede was news. Then there was the case of the man who was murdered in Kashmir; the case of a girl, aged fifteen, who'd been seen naked at a window; page 3, £6 a head for a film show; article about passion wagons. Then there were pictures of three pairs of naked Malayan ladies. And so forth. This obviously shows that there is a particular slant.

*Somerfield* You have not gone through the paper fairly. You have said nothing about a report on the war in the Congo, an article by the Archbishop of Canterbury, and another on cancer research. There were four pages of sport, a competition page, a women's page, and an entertainments page. You are being selective.

*Thorpe* Would you agree that there is more reference to sex and crime than you would find in some other newspapers?

*Somerfield* Yes, some of the other papers don't get the subject in the right proportion.

*Thorpe* But why is it a particularly important part of your newspaper? Is it because that is what sells the newspaper?

*Somerfield* You can't pick on one thing and say it sells newspapers. It all helps. One must produce a balanced newspaper, and that is what we aim to do.

*Thorpe* Well, it's an experiment that has succeeded.

*Somerfield* It's no experiment; it's been going on for a hundred years.

*Thorpe* Well, then it's no longer an experiment, it's something with which you are personally familiar — the effect of sex on a newspaper-readership figure.

*Somerfield* I am saying we do not ignore sex; it's an important part of life. We deal with other aspects of life as well.

*Mrs Hart* Mr Somerfield, quite clearly, the Diana Dors story and many of the other things that Jeremy has mentioned were things which would help sell the paper. Now can you tell me — if while you're having the serious contributions which you have mentioned to us — whether there are any limits beyond which you wouldn't go to try to sell your paper?

*Somerfield* The law looks after that. This is a point which the Press Council rather overlooks.

*Mrs Hart* But you would go as far as the law permits?

*Somerfield* The law is there as a safeguard.

I wasn't dissatisfied with that night's work as the publicity value was enormous. But I was dissatisfied with the fee. After no response from Granada, I wrote to them and got £500 for all the editors on the programme put together, and we gave it to a newspaper charity. Glancing at those names again, not one is an editor today — editors don't seem to last all that long.

That month we went ahead in the circulation race and the average for 1960 showed an increase for the first time for many years. To celebrate, the management put the price up, as they always seemed to do. Down went the sales, and the struggle started all over again.

I was next questioned on television about chequebook journalism. The Press Council were having their say about this and editors were sharply divided. The question was: should a newspaper pay for stories, or should they not? The amount does not affect the principle. I paid for stories because that was sometimes the only way to get them. The sum paid was controlled by the amount our rivals would pay and they were not above complaining bitterly if they were outbid. I saw nothing wrong with paying. The great majority of our contributors accepted money, including leading churchmen, lawyers, politicians and businessmen. We bought their words and their wisdom, and they knew we were going to sell them to the public. I see no difference between paying a saint or a sinner — sometimes the sinner's need is greater! I thought the complaint rubbish.

For some reason the Liberals liked 'having a go' at us at this time. David Steel wrote in the Guardian that we printed unsavoury evidence from the divorce courts. Since an Act of Parliament of 1926 expressly forbade this I took umbrage. I sharply replied that Mr Steel should know that a newspaper was permitted to print only the judge's summing-up. Would anyone claim that a newspaper should not print what a judge of the High Court has to say?

My attitude to the Press Council was clearly expressed in a leader we printed at the time of the Moors Murder Trial. One of our over-zealous reporters gave a witness money before the trial was concluded. But our fault was not as great as the then Attorney-General, Sir Elwyn Jones QC (afterwards Lord Chancellor) thought it was. He said we paid regular sums to the witness before he gave evidence. In fact we agreed to pay a lump sum after the trial, but during it the witness was in need, and our reporter gave him a few pounds to tide him over. It was kindly and foolish, but it was not a regular arrangement, and the motive was not bad.

An understanding Chief Superintendent from Scotland Yard came to see me officially. Many Yard men came unofficially. He framed his questions carefully, and told me not to say anything more than I needed to. You may be sure I did not and that I spoke in the presence of our solicitor. I sought out our retained counsel who was in the High Court at the time. He came out into the corridor to see me and I told him the story. 'My God,' he said, 'you've done it this time.' He was more worried than I was.

Both Houses of Parliament and the Press Council criticized us, but I felt the Council was piling it on and didn't intend doing much about it. But, for once, counsel really did 'have the wind up'. When everything blew over he kept telling me how lucky I'd been not to have gone to gaol. Perhaps he was right, though there were occasions when I thought a short spell inside might have been more restful than the office. And I had always wanted to write a column from the Tower. Like John Wilkes, I wanted a band to play me there.

The Press Council published a three-point Declaration of Principle, and we were prepared to agree to the first two points, which banned payment to witnesses before completion of a trial, but we wouldn't go along with the third, which sought to ban payment altogether to persons engaged in crime or other notorious misbehaviour where the public interest does not warrant it. Who was to decide what was notorious behaviour and what was in the public interest, other than ourselves? The Press Council went on to deplore publication of personal articles of an unsavoury nature by persons who have been concerned in criminal acts of vicious conduct. This was a blatant attempt to muzzle the Press, and we rejected it. Our leader, a classic of its kind, stated:

It is the duty of a newspaper to seek out and publish news

and information of public interest, and especially, at times, information which some people may wish suppressed. In pursuing that duty a newspaper may have to pay for the information it seeks. There have been countless cases where investigation by reporters has been of the greatest assistance to the police. The problems of what payments may be properly made, what persons may properly be questioned, is one which constantly engages the attention of journalists.

The News of the World believes that the Press Council has rendered a service to newspapers generally in laying down a code of conduct in respect of these matters, in relation to criminal proceedings. We regret, however, that the Council did not confine itself to matters, which, according to published record, arose during the Moors trial, and that it should have extended its Declaration to include an entirely unrelated matter. We do not believe that the public interest is served by the Council's trying to impose a general restriction in advance — above and beyond the present limitations of the law and the condemnation of the public if they err — on the judgement of editors as to what they may or may not publish.

In our view that is another step on the road to censorship. The public interest demands that matters which are criminal, vicious and unsavoury, should be exposed and not concealed. The greater the evil, the greater the need for exposure.

Although one understands that some people want to keep stories out of the newspapers for all sorts of reasons, some good, some bad, I believe that censorship of any kind is a great evil. The dictator countries proved that. Our inflexible rule was that the only consideration must be: is the news worth publishing, is it right to publish it and is it within the law to publish it? Even members of the staff, even an Editor's son, did not escape.

When an editor starts to leave out news and comment because someone presses him to do so, he should get another job. There are few exceptions. One is when the State is in peril, another when the suffering caused is unjust. But these few occasions must be watched closely. Even the 'D' notice system, by which a newspaper is restricted in what it prints, should be most carefully looked at. Governments are not above trying to impose censorship when it is convenient for them to do so. Neither they nor anyone else, should be allowed to get away with it.

# 17 Man at the Top

What sort of man was William Emsley Carr, Chairman of the News of the World? He was a proud man; proud of his grandfather, Lascelles, who bought the paper in 1891, and proud of his father, Emsley, who was Editor for half a century. At first, however, he was insecure and it took him time to reach full stature. He was not always an easy man to work with, for he could be tough and, especially after lunch, he could be rude. But he had the great quality of loyalty to the paper and to his staff, and that, in my eyes, was above everything else. If he sacked anyone, which he did rarely, he did it with the greatest reluctance and hated doing it. Some found him difficult to get close to, they thought him standoffish and cold. In fact he was a shy man, and, underneath, he really concerned himself about his friends and helped many quietly. His great qualities overshadowed all else. I saw him through the years in robust health and in sickness, and when ill he never complained, though the pain he endured was terrible. He was a brave man.

He was a connoisseur of Scotch whisky and was bold at the gambling tables. I've seen him win, and lose, thousands. Once, in Cannes, we worked a modest system at roulette that actually made money, but that was child's play to him. He liked the big table. On another occasion, at Vichy, where we'd gone to take the waters (and actually did for a week) he lost every penny we had with us — cash, travellers' cheques, the lot. I had to cable to London 'send century' to pay the hotel bill.

He suffered terribly from gout; once, when we drove through the battlefields of France sweat ran down his face. But he never complained, except to say I couldn't map-read, which, in fact, I could. After whisky and gambling, sport was his great passion, particularly golf and athletics, and he was knighted for his services to sport. He loved to play with Henry Cotton at Walton Heath, and to meet the other great sportsmen of the day.

People reacted strongly to him. They either liked him very much or disliked him a great deal. Some of the latter couldn't stand his criticism and chaff. But Bill Carr seldom took umbrage, nor did he bear malice.

I once wrote a letter of protest to him about his behaviour, but he tore it to pieces and bought me a bottle of champagne. New cars were twice ordered for me when he'd been really too diabolical. I could put up with this because of his newspaper flair, his friendship in times of trouble, and because he had tremendous respect for the position of the Editor, probably because his father held the job for fifty years. No one but himself was allowed to criticise the Editor, and once, when another director sat in the Editor's chair, only because it was a convenient place to sit at the time, Carr ordered him out, saying 'I've never sat in that chair'. It was his father's.

Before lunch he was a brilliant mathematician, and could do sums on the back of one of the cigarette packets he was never without — more quickly than experts with sliderules. As one who always made mistakes adding up a modest expense sheet, I was astonished by his skill. With the exception of the editorial, with which he never interfered, he knew in detail the working of the many companies he controlled, particularly their financial position.

Whether he made errors of judgement in some of the big deals in which the company was engaged I do not know; but I do know that he always took the blame on his own broad shoulders. As the boss he thought that that was the right thing and he minded about the right thing. We had what a psychologist might call a 'love-hate relationship' which changed to warm regard when we were both retired. He stuck by me through thick and thin; and I by him.

Bill Carr was essentially a Fleet Street man and many are the stories told about him. Some are true, some not. It is said, for example, that he emerged from the Savoy after one of his many lunch-time sessions, got into a taxi and said to the cabbie 'Home Cleaver'. Cleaver, his chauffeur, was sitting in the Bentley further up the street. It led to a slight misunderstanding.

I was there, close to midnight, in the Savoy when Chapman-Walker and Carr had an argument. Bill, claiming that only the Prime Minister could decide, told me to ring Downing Street immediately and make an appointment with the Prime Minister, Sir Alec Douglas-Home. I did so and we were told to go to 10 Downing Street at ten o'clock next morning, by the back entrance. It was thought inappropriate that we should be seen in Downing Street, as it was not an official call.

When we arrived outside the back door, I was green; it had been a heavy night. The others didn't say how they were feeling. Carr never had a hangover, so he said.

Before we could discuss the object of our visit together we were whisked into the Cabinet room. In came the Prime Minister with his advisers, and we were asked to be seated. The Prime Minister sat facing us in the middle of the long table. I'd once been told that Lloyd George had made love on that table and I tried to imagine exactly where. My mind was wandering.

Sir Alec bade us good morning and asked why we wished to see him, which was reasonable. Silence. Then Chapman-Walker, quick as a flash — he was always good in a crisis — said: 'The situation, Prime Minister.' Sir Alec responded: 'Could you define that a little more closely?' I jerked back to earth. 'Rhodesia, sir,' I said.

The Prime Minister took the ball immediately and ran swiftly with it, much to my and perhaps the others' relief. At the end of the discourse he looked encouragingly at us. Carr then came in strongly: 'May I suggest, Prime Minister, that you don't wear those half-moon glasses when you next appear on television, it gives you a wrong image.' Sir Alec gravely thanked him and then, with his characteristic quizzical smile, said: 'Perhaps a little refreshment, gentlemen.' I sighed with relief.

Back on Horse Guard Parade I looked with bloodshot eyes at the Chairman who never seemed any different, lucky chap, and said: 'Don't you ever do that to me again.' We made for the office.

Carr had many brilliant and staggering publicity ideas. We were lunching at the 'canteen', as we called the Savoy Grill. 'Hire a ship,' he said, 'run a competition and take the winners on a cruise.' I thought he meant a boat on the river. But no, he meant the *Queen Mary*!

It was an unusual experience to ring up Cunard and say: 'What would it cost to hire the *Queen Mary* for the weekend?' They were surprised too. Anyway, we hired it and took a thousand readers to Las Palmas for Christmas. The steward said it was the best trip ever for tips, which taught me something about the spending power of our readers. Many were seasick, but Carr loved it. I drank champagne and he drank whisky and we sang 'A little ship was on the sea' as the waves smashed over the ship, causing no little damage.

Some danced the night through; Tom Jones, a popular director, lost his teeth; they smashed on the washroom floor. Joe Davis, the world snooker champion, broke his braces while dancing and his trousers came down. It was a remarkable cruise.

Carr drove his sports car like the wind, and I read the latest book to him as we travelled to our companies in the provinces. I was glad to read, for although he was a most skilful driver, 100 mph doesn't suit me. I wrote speeches for him which he tore up. One he strangled to death in public. 'It says here', he said, 'that this is a joke. I don't see it.' As he read it, it wasn't.

When my wife and I stayed with Sir William and Lady Carr at the Majestic at Cannes we rarely saw the sea. The routine was champagne with orange juice before lunch, a long lunch, a little sleep, change for dinner, over to the Casino, and back in the small hours to the hotel. Among the many good ideas that emerged there was a highly successful magazine that we bought.

Carr always had ideas, some good, some hair-raising. 'You can't win 'em all,' he would say. 'Don't be afraid to get your feet wet.' Some failed to catch fire, but others were top-class.

So, that was Bill Carr, talented, shy, tough, bold, loyal, generous, unpredictable and brave, but above all a News of the World man. His sense of humour was not sly, quick or sophisticated. He told jokes so tediously that they were no longer jokes. He was a contradiction, but he had guts, even when he was close to death. And he always had ideas.

# 18 Meeting Top People

When there was an opportunity to travel or get out on a story, I took it. A journalist, even an Editor, must look about and see what's going on. Gerard Fairlie, one of our distinguished correspondents, went with me to Paris and Rome to see Bridget Bardot and the Pope — on different days, I hasten to add.

Bridget gave us a great story and we gave her flowers. I shall never forget the way she sat on the floor, crossed-legged, and stood up without effort and without using her hands or arms. Try it! A French lawyer friend helped us to get this series. He was an amusing man. He described how the Gestapo came to take him in Paris during the war. 'My mistress and I were in bed in this room,' he said. 'There was a knock on the door. We knew it would be the Gestapo. I told the girl to ring my wife and tell her to get her boyfriend to bring the car to the place we had arranged. It's urgent.' He escaped and deserved to.

I played it softly, softly with Pope John, because my head was singing. The night before, Fairlie and I had tried to get a horse through the revolving doors of my Rome hotel. He wanted some sugar. It's very hard to get a horse through revolving doors. The first part gets through, but the rest sticks. We gave him the sugar though, paid the cabbie who owned the horse — or so he said — and got to bed at 4 am. We were not unhappy. At six Fairlie rang to say that the Pope could see me and my wife first thing. Why, oh why must I always have a hangover on important occasions?

We got to the Vatican in time and Pope John was delightful, like an egg in an egg cup, wearing a red hat. He told me that St Paul was the greatest of all reporters. I had to tell his Holiness that my father would turn in his grave if he saw me talking to him. 'Why?' he asked. 'Because he was a Methodist local preacher.' The Pope's shoulders shook. My wife disgraced herself. She asked the interpreter a charming and good-looking man, whether it was true that priests were celibate. He admitted as much. 'What a waste', she murmured.

But we didn't joke throughout the conversation. The Pope talked seriously to me about my responsibilities as an Editor. Then he loaded my wife with medals and beads. They got on famously. Pope John was a great man. Even I, a lapsed Methodist, would have followed him. The best remark ever attributed to him was the one he gave in answer to the question: 'How many people work in the Vatican?' 'About 50 per cent,' he replied. Just like a newspaper office.

From the sublime to the ridiculous. I wrote a story about a dog — most dog stories go well. Mr Macmillan made a choice comment when the Russians sent their first astronaut to London, the one who followed a dog into space. The streets were choked with people. 'Thank God,' said the Prime Minister, 'they didn't send the dog. The crowds would have gone mad.'

But my dog was different. He had but one testicle; what dog breeders call a monorched and the question was: should he be used at stud? 'Why not,' I said. 'If he can manage it?' And he could. The Kennel Club held an enquiry about monorchids. I told the story to an old friend who had become Lord Donovan, a great lawyer, famous for the Donovan report. He sent me a written judgement:

My dear Stafford:
What fun you do have … How useful for us all to know how to verify that our testicles are genuine! And what fresh hopes would be kindled in some of us to know how to get new ones. Obviously you must go to extremes to get in on the enquiry. Should not a High Court Judge, for

example, conduct the enquiry, not just a mere QC? Otherwise I can't think of anything you can do, unless you can disguise some member of your staff as a shaggy dog and offer his own genuine pair as exhibits for comparison. Anyway, good luck to you, and I shall watch out for the sequel with genital, I mean genuine, interest.

Yours ever, Terence.

Who said judges don't have a sense of humour?

The News of the World had a lot of friends, particularly judges. They read the paper, they said, to see what sentences their brothers were awarding. The 'trade paper,' they called it. Mr Justice Cassels, a reporter before he was a judge, said we were always accurate. He was known to delay his summing up until the News of the World man was in the Press box. He never forgot what made a good story.

There was a great flurry the day the drug squad raided my flat and searched it for dope. We were running a campaign against some pop-singers at the time, and someone unknown retaliated by saying that drugs were to be found at my address. The police officers didn't make any further enquiries. They barged in, flashing a warrant. My wife was unconcerned. 'My husband takes pills for pills,' she joked. Then she said: 'I must phone the News of the World'. 'Why?' 'Because my husband is the Editor.' 'Jesus Christ,' exclaimed the sergeant. 'Not quite,' said Dibbie enjoying herself, 'though I must admit he sometimes behaves like that.' 'This is no joking matter,' said the cops, hurrying away.

The upshot was that the detectives were given the job of guarding the flat all day and night, in case any other false stories were spread. They made themselves at home, brewed up, fried up and drank whisky. Eventually I got their chief to call them off, on the ground that I couldn't afford them any longer.

One Saturday night, when the dope story was running,

thousands filled Bouverie Street and tried to keep our loaded paper vans from leaving. The City Police were out in force and we were ready to repel boarders. There were some scuffles, and I saw more than one youth fly through the air into a police van. One got such a back-hander from the constable who was guarding the front door that he took no further interest in the demonstration. I congratulated the officer. 'I saw nothing,' he said. It wasn't long before our vans were on the move again.

The event pleased me a great deal. The young were responding to what we had to say. It is the only occasion I recall of a demonstration against a newspaper. Naturally I had to phone one or two other editors and ask them to take their readers away from our front door.

I interviewed Edna Kalman, the head girl of a vice-gang, who instructed the other girls in the arts and crafts of the business. Edna had one thousand customers a year for several years. I thought this an interesting social phenomenon. She served tea most delicately, crooking her little finger, as in Kensington, and she was really shocked by outspoken language. Her story was frank, down to earth and rather sad. She took our money for her story about the gang, gave up her business and bred dogs.

One of the detectives on the case discovered that the gang got to know the moves he intended to take. He made telephone calls with the utmost discretion and met me in places where it was unlikely we would be seen. We helped the Yard. One of their problems was to track down the birth certificates of the villains. Were they Italian or Maltese? It was important to know. Noyes Thomas, a brilliant reporter, found the answer in Malta. Tommy wrote many fine stories and his best, I think, was his report from Japan on the horror of the atom bombs. He was among the first to enter the devastated cities.

As the Press Council had knocked us about, I thought it

might be amusing to complain to it for a change. 'A lot of newspapers,' I wrote, tongue in cheek, 'are using four letter words — not the News of the World. Do you think we should give them in our court reports? They are often used, but we have regard to delicacy and good form and do not print them.' This was in reference to the Lady Chatterley trial, during which Counsel spoke in the frankest terms about the activities of the lady and the gamekeeper.

I said I was shocked, and I really did think it pretty rough. I certainly would not have printed the words. The Press Council took my letter seriously. They were not in favour of four-letter words, they said. It was duly reported that I had asked for guidance and our high moral tone was favourably commented upon.

When Queen Ena of Spain's 'life' was on offer I sent a reporter by plane with her favourite dish — smoked salmon. Not just a pound or so, but a whole fish, and a big one at that. She was hooked, and our man came back with the manuscript leaving the opposition to wonder why.

Then there was the night the office caught fire. We had put the paper to bed and I thought I deserved a little relaxation. A girl-friend had a convenient flat, so I took myself there, leaving my deputy in charge. I was nicely tucked up when the phone rang. 'The office is on fire.' It was a joke, of course, I thought. I'd left my phone number with instructions to be called only in an emergency. 'Go away,' I said, or words to that effect. After a short interval the phone rang again. 'I'm not kidding, it really is on fire.'

I threw on my clothes. There was no taxi available, so I ran from Charing Cross to Bouverie Street, where the whole building was blazing. Hours later, after the fire brigade and police had done their stuff, we all had a drink in my room. It was mid-day Sunday. Suddenly I saw the managing director's eyes riveted on my ankles. I'd forgotten to put my socks on!

Years later I crossed the Atlantic to see the girl who

owned the flat. Just before the boat got to Vancouver I was smitten with gout. I hobbled down the gangway. She stepped forward to greet me. 'My God,' she said, 'you've aged.' I knew then that it was time for me to settle down.

Nancy Spain came to us from the Express and took on any reporting job given her. She was no prima donna, as some not as talented often are. She started her first column: 'Mother always said I would end up in the News of the World.' She covered a leek show way up in the North-East and started her report: 'Then in came a man with the biggest one I'd ever seen.' Nancy would sing war-time songs with the boys in the pub outside our back door, and she knew all the words. She was a lovable creature.

One day we were in the Savoy, it might just as well have been Mick's Cafe, and I happened to say it was my birthday. She took off her cufflinks, chunky gold ones, set with precious stones, which she had bought in South America. 'They're yours,' she said. Next day I sent them back; they were too expensive to keep. I wish I hadn't. Shortly after that I asked her to cover the Grand National. She flew to Liverpool in a small plane that crashed and she was killed on the racecourse. I read the lesson at her funeral, or at least tried to, for the page in my shaking fingers wouldn't turn over and I choked.

Our political writers were the best in Fleet Street. After Winston Churchill came his son, Randolph. We also had John Freeman, Nye Bevan and Bob Boothby. Boothby's copy, in his copper-plate handwriting, was never late, was rarely too long and was always on the target. The Chairman and I had a sharp disagreement about one of his articles. While I was on holiday, Carr and Professor Jackson between them removed Bob's article from the paper. I was furious. How dare they interfere in an editorial matter? They said Bob agreed to take a strong line about Germany and didn't do so. My line was that it was none of their business, my deputy was in charge in my absence, and they had no right to lean on him. No Editor of the News of the World had ever been subjected to this sort of pressure. Carr and I were still arguing about that twenty-five years after.

Boothby got an interview with Hitler. He entered the Führer's study and walked the long distance towards the desk. 'It seemed a mile away,' said Bob. 'As I approached, Hitler stood up, gave the Nazi salute and shouted "Heil Hitler". I saluted and exclaimed "Heil Boothby".'

Bob told me this story about an action he took for libel and was awarded large damages out of court. His counsel questioned him closely. 'You will be cross-examined about your personal life,' he said. 'Tell me the answer to this question, but think about it first. "Have you ever done anything you are ashamed of?" ' Boothby replied: 'No need to think about it — all the time, never stopped.'

When I was in one of my resigning moods, Boothby was one of the people who persuaded me to stay. He once put two bottles of brandy on my table with a message: 'Stay put.' It was my wedding day, but after the ceremony I went to work, drank black velvet at the Press Club, missed the boat-train and arrived in France for my honeymoon a day late. My wife had driven to Dover, put the car on the boat and waited on the quay at Calais. When I arrived, she was not best pleased. 'Where have you been?' 'Putting the paper to bed.' 'I thought you were going to put me to bed.' Some day I may live this down.

Nye Bevan was a brilliant talker but not a good writer. 'The Bollinger Bolshevik' could make people hoot with mirth and then write a dreary article. Nye had met Kruschev in Russia and he described his eating habits — something akin to Henry VIII's — and his temper. It was great stuff. But he couldn't put it across in the written word.

When returning from El Vinos it was found that Nye's large, shining, black car was in the way of the newspaper vans. A packer cursed Bevan for leaving his car in the way. 'Just what to expect from a bloody capitalist.' he shouted.

Randolph Churchill could write brilliantly when he wanted to, but not always on the subject one had agreed on. When he went to South Africa he got himself detained but not for what he wrote: in the space for signature or thumb-print on the entry document, he put his thumb-print. He would go purple in the face and bang the table for no apparent reason. Derek Jackson would do the same.

I saw Randolph crash his fist on the table in the Savoy, knocking over the coffee cups and the brandy glasses, because Carr had said quite innocently: 'When in Paris meeting de Gaulle, have a word with Lord Warwick who is there, he's a friend and knows about French politics.' Randolph blew his top and roared: 'Do you think he knows more about French politics than I do?' and waltzed out of the room. 'What did I say?' said the mystified Carr.

I visited Randolph's home at East Bergholt in Suffolk, and we sat on the terrace with our drinks. It was a beautiful day and the garden was lovely. 'You know about dogs?' said Randolph to my wife. 'Look at those beautiful Pug puppies.' Dibbie did know about dogs and she looked doubtful. Randolph went on about the pups; one was going to a stately home, another to an ambassador and so on. 'Well they won't get Pugs,' said Dibbie. Randolph spluttered, and when Dibbie asked if he had any other dogs, replied 'Yes, a King Charles.' 'That,' said my wife 'is the answer.' Randolph went crimson in the face. 'It's not true,' he roared, 'he's too much of a gentleman.'

Another time we talked until the cook got cross and went home. Randolph was a brilliant conversationalist, especially about his youth and the famous men who came to dinner with his father: F. E. Smith, Lloyd George and others. Eventually we went in to a burnt offering and all there was left to do was to drink. Randolph put on the Tom Lehrer record 'We'll all fry together when we fry'. It was the time of the Aldermaston marches and the atom bomb rumpus. I went to bed. In the morning I crawled down. There was no one about, light were still blazing, the french windows open and the wind was blowing the curtains into the room. I crept out, found my car and drove away.

When I had the temerity to suggest that it was not the moment for him to go to the United States, Randolph sent me this telegram: 'Why don't you want me to go to Washington? What the hell has it got to do with you? I don't mind where you go, and would not have the insolence to make any suggestions. Pray understand this: I am an independent person, and shall go where I like and write what I think. You may have the power to suppress what I write, but you cannot yet, in a free community, restrict my movements. Pray remember that I am not a hack.'

What Randolph had momentarily forgotten was that the paper was paying for the trip. A little thing like that made no difference to him. He called me a 'yellow-bellied coward' on the telephone. Even if he were right, I felt it wasn't quite the way for the political correspondent to speak to the Editor. He had to go. But he beat me to it and sacked himself, shouting 'I won't write for your bloody awful paper'.

You couldn't help liking him because he could have such a charming way when he felt like it. He planted a tree in his garden in memory of one of my visits, poured champagne over the roots, raised his glass and said: 'Let's drink to the tree; when it's grown and we are old, we'll sit under it and talk about life and people.' But he didn't get old. I was sad about that. 'I'll put a candle in the window for you,' he used to say.

Randolph's last telegram to me read: 'Freedom of the press does not mean freedom for proprietors or editors to suppress the truth as written for them by their gifted correspondents. Please reflect on this. Regards, Randolph.'

It was meeting great personalities that gave me the keenest pleasure, not only the politicians, but the top sportsmen of the day. I would sometimes get up before dawn and drive to Marlborough to meet Gordon Richards who was in charge of our horses and to see Scobie Breasly 'ride work'. Ritchie Benaud was a brilliant talker about cricket, so were Joe Davis, Frank Swift on their sports, and Frank Butler was an outstanding Sports Editor. After politicians, sportsmen fascinated me more than any other group.

We organised dinner parties at our headquarters in Cliveden Place, near Sloane Square, and everyone who was anybody came to them: Edward Heath, Harold Wilson, Jeremy Thorpe, Harold Macmillan; business men, like David Barran, then head of Shell; Henry Cotton and other sportsmen; top men in the law, Lords Devlin, Donovan, Hailsham and Shawcross. The Marquis of Exeter was the best talker, Jeremy Thorpe the most amusing, Bob Boothby the most outspoken.

George Brown was different. He once arrived late, not in a dinner jacket like everyone else. I had put him next to Mark Chapman-Walker, our managing director. George, knowing that Mark had at one time worked at the Conservative Central Office, said that he wouldn't sit next to a 'Tory stooge.' Stupidly, instead of telling him to sit in his place or nowhere, we all moved round. George got crosser and crosser and eventually tapped the Chairman on the chest and said: 'We will remember you, brother.' 'I'm not your brother,' said Carr. I took George down in the lift and saw him to his car. 'We'll show the buggers,' he said. As I helped him in the car I said: 'I'm one of the buggers; I'm just seeing you to your car.' It was impossible not to like George.

A short story came in about a workman striking through a water main with his pick and causing water to spurt over shoppers. A young northern sub-editor, who handled it, put up the headline, 'Workman's pick causes flood'. The Chief Sub advised him to change it; he could see a misprint looming up. After a pause, a look of understanding crossed over the young man's face. 'You're quite right,' he said, without a smile. 'Change it to tool will you?'

# 19 Inside Murder

I wrote the life story of Haigh, the acid bath murderer, who shot and then dumped Mrs Durand Deacon into a tub of acid at Crawley, Sussex. He 'treated' a number of others the same way.

I got close to Haigh and found that his background was religious, gloomy and restricted. His mother was ashamed when she conceived him because she had, she told me, 'sinned' with her own husband. When I took her a bunch of roses she said, 'you're just like my son; sit there in his chair'. I hoped I wasn't like George. He was a cold-hearted little man who murdered without the slightest regret. He was a liar and mean. His last gift to his girlfriend was a typewriter, and I had to get it out of pawn.

But the story behind the story was fascinating. I got it by sitting in the bar at the White Hart in Lewes and sending Haigh a reply-paid telegram reading: 'Wire me and I'll come and see you. Will make an interesting offer.' I organised his defence and got Sir David Maxwell Fife, afterwards Lord Kilmuir, and Lord Chancellor and Mr G. R. F. Morris, afterwards Judge Gwyn Morris QC of the Old Bailey to defend him. We knew that Sir Hartley Shawcross, Attorney General at that time, would prosecute. The idea of ex-Attorney (Fife) against the current one (Shawcross) appealed to both Haigh and me.

Mr Justice Humphreys, who later sold us his famous cases, was determined to add Haigh to his list. When Haigh came up before Humphreys at Lewes Assizes we weren't ready with the defence and asked to go to the Old Bailey, where Humphreys was due to sit. He agreed. At the Old Bailey we still weren't ready and asked that the case be put back. But Humphreys wasn't sitting at the Old Bailey next time. 'Certainly not,' he said, 'the case must go back to Lewes; it should never have come to the Old Bailey.' Did he forget that he sent it there and did he not know he was sitting at the next Lewes Assizes? I have no doubts. He eventually condemned Haigh to death.

I saw Haigh at Wandsworth the night before he was hanged and we had a remarkable conversation. 'What shall I do on my last night?' he asked. 'Write me a letter,' I said, 'It will go well with the story.' He agreed. 'I don't suppose you will,' I said. 'You're not suggesting I would lie about a thing like that,' said this smiling, little monster. 'I never tell lies.'

When I suggested that he read a book, he replied: 'Certainly, what do you suggest, something not too long; it would be maddening if I was at an interesting point when they send for me.' I sent him, by special messenger, a Neville Cardus book on cricket. It should have been called 'Close of Play'. Haigh gave me a list of things he wanted me to do: to see his mother, his girlfriend; send his suit to Madame Tussaud's. I felt sick for months and, for the first time in my life, took sleeping pills. Haigh had no conscience at all; it might have been removed by surgical operation. He had no regrets, but was brave about death, joking about being hanged and asking what he should say to God when he arrived in the next world. He even suggested: 'Sorry I dropped in like this.'

Mr Justice Humphreys was right to condemn him to death according to the law at that time, but I didn't like the way he dealt with our defence witness, Dr Yellowlees, the psychiatrist, who said that Haigh was mad, which he undoubtedly was. I had found it difficult to get a pyschiatrist to say this. I approached several, who went to see Haigh, charged fifty guineas and then said he was sane.

'My dear boy,' said Junior Counsel, 'You're going about it the wrong way. Be a bit of a psychiatrist yourself. Say to the next one you see, "many of your colleagues have said

Haigh is sane," and then reel off the names of those who have been to gaol to interview him.' It worked. Said Dr Yellowlees: 'If they say he's sane, he must be mad.' And so he reported. Unhappily he made a poor witness, for he couldn't recall how many times he went to the prison to see Haigh, and guessed wrongly. Sir Hartley destroyed him: 'If you can't be sure about that, what can you be sure about?' Summing up to the jury, the judge dealt with Yellowlees like this: 'We now come to the evidence of Dr Yellowlees; do you believe that?' His voice rose sharply. When we studied the transcript, with an appeal in mind, there was no fault to be found with the words. A tape-recording would have given a much fairer indication of tone and emphasis.

Haigh had stayed in an hotel in Kensington where his victims also lived. In his old age, Humphreys went to stay at the same hotel. Did he occupy the same room? I could never discover, but the idea is spine-chilling.

I once wrote that I thought you could get too close to a killer, and the idea worried me. It didn't affect Norman Rae, our crime man, however. He took Haigh's coat off the stand in my room and tried it for size. 'Nice coat,' he said: 'I'll have it. He's got no further use for it.' And he walked out with it on his back.

Bolam, the Editor of the Daily Mirror went to prison for contempt of court over the Haigh case. Before the trial his paper described Haigh as a monster, and the Lord Chief Justice, Lord Goddard, was scathing in his criticism. I was much concerned about this as we were paying for Haigh's defence. I tried to put pressure on Haigh, saying there was no point in complaining about the Mirror, for his story was that he was mad and drank the blood of his victims, which is broadly what the Mirror said.

But Haigh was adamant. He made his complaint and the court had to act. Undoubtedly the Mirror was at fault, but the ridiculous thing was that the Editor was still in prison when, at the trial, Haigh's counsel pleaded for him on the same lines as the Mirror story.

Haigh was hanged, but there is no question of his trial having been prejudiced in any way.

Bolam took his prison sentence sadly and I don't believe that he ever recovered from it. Another feature of the contempt case was the way in which the Lord Chief Justice sent for the Mirror directors. They filed into court, looking sheepish and he 'tore the wool off' them. I always took the line that I would never go to court against my will unless arrested. If I were arrested I had to be charged. Our lawyers never gave me a satisfactory answer on this one; fortunately it was never put to the test.

The Recorder of London once sent for me to 'tick me off' for an article about the Old Bailey that he didn't care about. I said I wasn't fond of the Old Bailey and would he meet me at the Savoy? He didn't want to do this, but asked whether I would take tea in his private room. To this I agreed, and we got on very well. I agreed to publish a reply, which I was glad to do in line with our policy of giving everybody a fair shout.

We are fortunate to live in a country where, even today, the rights of the citizen are regarded as being of the greatest importance. The young are not grateful enough to those who fought through the centuries for their freedom. The present-day tendency to defy the law is madness. Of course, if the News of the World uncovered any blatant fault by the police, we demanded the whole truth about it and raised the matter at the highest level, but generally we have been on the side of the police and have supported them. But, unfortunately, there are always a few black sheep.

I was only once arrested. The police found me trying to get into a London flat. It was my step-son's, and I had difficulty with the key which I had never used before. The problem arose because two fingers were blown off my right hand during the war. I was taken to the police station and charged with being drunk.

I denied it, saying I had been to a party but was well able to call a cab and get myself to the flat. I asked permission to telephone my doctor, who was treating me for diabetes and blood pressure, and my solicitor. This was refused, and I did not take that refusal lightly as it was my right to make the calls.

The official police instruction says: 'Any person in custody will be allowed to speak on the telephone to his solicitor, or to his friends, provided that no hindrance is reasonably likely to be caused in the process of investigation or the administration of justice by his so doing.' This order is to be found on the reverse of Form 59 issued by the Metropolitan Police, and should always be carried out.

Three witnesses said I left the party in good order and my doctor said the drugs he had prescribed for me would cause me to stagger. The magistrate dismissed the case and awarded me £20 costs against the police. This was a trivial incident, but the refusal of the police to let me telephone my solicitor even the next morning, bothered me and I took the best advice available in London on whether an action lay for wrongful arrest, for refusing to allow me to call my doctor and solicitor and for locking me up for the night.

Counsel's answer was no. It all turned on the question: did the police have reason to believe I was drunk? The fact that it had been found to the contrary was of no avail. This is wrong. In a survey conducted in 1972 by the *Criminal Law Review* it was revealed that of 134 defendants selected at random, 74 per cent of those who asked to see a solicitor were not allowed to do so. Decent citizens, and they are the vast majority, support the police, of that I am certain, but when they act unfairly they make enemies needlessly.

My case turned on my inability to open the front door of the flat. I showed the magistrate my damaged hand. 'How did that happen?' he asked. My reply was rather embarrassing: 'Fighting for my King and Country.' The beak replied: 'The police might have helped this gentleman.' He awarded me costs.

They didn't go far: only, in fact, to the Wig and Pen in Fleet Street.

# 20 Christine Keeler

The Christine Keeler story was the greatest of my time. It had everything — sex, intrigue, espionage, politics, high society, crime, passion, the law. You name it. And did it get me into trouble? You can say that again! And a lot of other people too.

The Chairman, Sir William Carr, came into my room, shut the door carefully, and looked behind the curtains, before whispering: 'Make some very discreet enquiries about a scandal involving a girl and a Minister.' 'I have,' I said, opening a drawer in my desk and passing over three thousand typewritten words. Peter Earle, one of our most astute crime reporters, had been busy.

However, I decided against printing it straight away as I wanted the girl's own story. Sir William had a higher sense of duty. Although, like me, his concern was for the paper, he was also concerned about the Government. We talked it over with Mark Chapman-Walker and decided that Mark, former Tory backroom boy, should see the Prime Minister, Mr MacMillan, and tell him all. I was against it, but was overruled. My one thought was to keep the story to ourselves, but Carr and Chapman-Walker decided that it was too big for that.

I shall not tell the Keeler story again, for millions of words have been written about it and the innocent have suffered enough. Sometimes this can't be helped, but all the sympathy in this affair has been one way. The men involved in this case were experienced men of the world; Christine Keeler was young, and although certainly not innocent, not nearly as sophisticated as others concerned. The girl had been exploited all her life. She had not the slightest idea that her role would topple a Government; others should have done.

The Labour Opposition used Keeler remorselessly. It claimed that security was threatened, although it knew it never was. It knew it was unlikely that the Minister involved told Keeler state secrets in bed. Did it matter all that much that a Russian spy also jumped between her sheets? The Opposition saw its chance to use the girl to knock the Government and didn't miss a trick.

The Minister helped the Socialists by lying to Parliament about his association with the girl, but was it so unusual for a Minister to lie to the House? Even Sir Stafford Cripps, a former Labour Chancellor of the Exchequer and most upright man, lied about devaluation. When is a lie not a lie? The Minister lied to spare his wife embarrassment. I know of worse things. He was stupid. If he had told the truth, everyone would have forgiven him; he would have gone to the back benches and returned to the Government in due course. We really are a race of hypocrites. It is not unknown for a Minister, even a Prime Minister, even a President of the United States, to have a mistress.

A French editor came to see me and asked about the affair. 'A Minister,' I said, 'had a mistress.' 'Yes,' he said. I went on: 'He lied about it, to his wife and to his colleagues.' 'But of course.' 'Well, our politicians are upset about it.' The Frenchman looked perplexed: 'How very droll,' he said. That just about sums it up.

Perhaps some will say that I exploited the girl by printing her story. If that is so, at least we paid her £20,000 for the privilege. The story put on thousands of copies, and it ranks as one of the greatest political tragedies.

Our reporters, Peter Earle and Noyes Thomas, spent a lot of time with Christine. She kept her word and told us everything. This was my general experience: those considered outside the pale usually kept their word, even if the agreements with them were made on the backs of envelopes, while others of better breeding and education are not always so trustworthy.

Christine was amusing and good company. Her friend, Mandy Rice Davies, was bright and as sharp as a needle. I recall her in the reporters' room, surrounded by our keen young men. She was good to look at and they looked. Her phrase in the witness box, when told that her account of events was denied by the men involved, will live. 'They would, wouldn't they?' I heard an ex-minister quote the same words years later when talking about the trade unions.

Of course the Press Council had a rush of blood to the head about it. Once again I'd let the side down by revealing to the general public what really went on. But I didn't believe in keeping history dark. Naturally I was grilled on television. Most, it seemed, had sympathy for the Minister. Rightly so, but what about the girl? As she wrote to The Times: 'I have a right to tell my side of the story.' She certainly had.

My sin, I was told, was to tell the story for commercial ends. But what is wrong with good, honest commercial ends? That is what the newspaper business is all about. My job of telling the truth was just as honourable as that of others who complained.

This all happened in 1963 and six years later we published Christine's book. All hell broke loose once again. I was kept away from television this time, and Rupert Murdoch, the new Australian Chairman, took over. David Frost crucified him. Murdoch said we printed the story to show up politicians who lied. It was untrue, a poor excuse and not needed. We printed the story to sell newspapers. I wanted to give Christine's side of the story, and she had one.

Murdoch said he took the decision to print and didn't wish to hide behind the Editor. He did not understand that, in this country the Editor is wholly responsible. That's his job. It was courageous of him to take responsibility, but he was wrong in his judgement and wrong to interfere with the way I wished to present the story.

In my view the Minister had suffered enough and there was no need at this time even to mention his name, Murdoch wrote me a note saying he was appalled by what I said in answer to Cardinal Heenan, who announced that he would not write an article for us, as he had agreed to do, because we had printed the Keeler story. The Daily Mail quoted me as replying: 'I'm surprised that the Cardinal doesn't want to preach to eighteen million sinners.' Murdoch told me he had apologised to the Cardinal, and I should remember that the News of the World had only one voice. 'That voice is mine,' he said.

I didn't care about anyone apologising for me, nor did I take kindly to the idea that I no longer had a voice. I had become used to having one. I went to see the Cardinal, who was charming and said he would give me ten minutes. We talked for an hour. I said I couldn't apologise, and he said there was no reason for me to do so; he thought I'd made a good point. Then he wisely remarked: 'We are, of course, all sinners.'

I put it to him that if a person of eminence, such as he, agreed to write for my paper — they often did — I wouldn't dream of issuing a public statement that I had withdrawn the offer. I would do so privately. He readily conceded the point, and said his concern was not to offend his faithful followers. I saw that and said that, had he explained privately, I would have understood and all would have passed off peacefully. He won me by his wisdom and his charm, and particularly by his comment: 'I've never heard of an Editor without a voice.' A great man.

Mr I. Stewart Cook of Windsor wrote: 'Every literate citizen in the country has heard of the Keeler series and the News of the World has got the most widespread free advertisement from both ITV and BBC.' I'm glad that at least one person recognised the object of the enterprise.

This is what the Press Council stated on 6 October 1963 after I bought the Keeler story:

The action of the News of the World in paying £23,000 for the confessions of Miss Keeler, and publishing in these articles details of her sordid life story, was particularly damaging to the morals of young people. By this exploiting vice and sex for commercial reward the News of the World has done a disservice both to the public welfare and to the Press.

How pompous is it possible to get?
I replied:

The Christine Keeler story is news, no newspaper has failed to recognize this. The only difference between the News of the World and other newspapers is that we were the first to publish material with an authentic basis. In order to provide the facts we had to pay. The complaints you mention appear to be mainly directed to the profits which accrue to unworthy persons who capitalize their notoriety. Such a criticism may in particular cases be perfectly valid, but when directed at this newspaper in this instance it is clearly misconceived. Does anyone suggest that the Christine Keeler story should have been suppressed? A healthy society must surely demand exposure, however sordid, in the context of recent events. Nothing published in the News of the World by way of comment has sought to disguise as virtue that which is vicious, but in the belief that the public is entitled to know what is going on, and to know authentically; we have discharged our prime duty of giving the news. A prodigious and mounting readership clearly acknowledges the rightness of the course we have taken.

The Press Council was ham-fisted. When we announced we were going to publish extracts from a book by Christine Keeler some time after the original story, it condemned us before the extracts appeared. It should, at least, have waited for publication. It seemed very much to me like the offence of loitering with intent to commit a felony before any crime occurs. This is what John Gordon, brilliant and acid columnist of the Sunday Express wrote:

> The declaration of the Press Council about the Christine Keeler memoir in the News of the World is pompous tommytosh. In my view, what a newspaper cares to print is its own business so long as it conforms to the law. Even if the tastes of its readers aren't mine or yours.
>
> But above all I think it an astonishing performance for the Council to find a newspaper guilty of publishing something reprehensible and against the public interest before it has published it. And therefore before the Council has any basis for deciding that it is against the public interest.

It seemed to me that the Press Council was determined to restrict us if they could. It invited me to attend a meeting to discuss the Keeler book, but I refused to go unless any charges against us were specifically stated.

They were not, but we were again censured.

It was becoming a habit. In getting a story we were always scrupulously correct and no complaint was ever made against us on that score. But when it came to what we printed I would allow no interference. It would be a bad day for newspapers and for the country if anybody, other than judges of the High Court on proper legal grounds, could stop a newspaper from printing, without malice, what it believed to be true and is prepared to back with evidence.

The boys got out a fake edition about me on my 59th birthday.

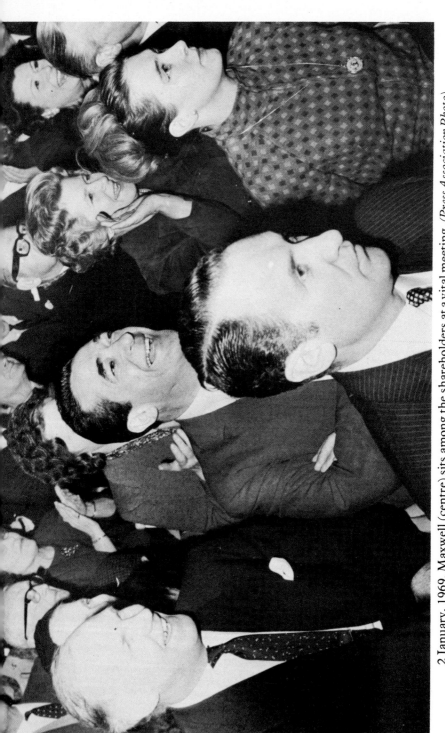

2 January, 1969. Maxwell (centre) sits among the shareholders at a vital meeting. *(Press Association Photo).*

# 21  As I Saw it

About this time I put down my views on the Press Council and newspapers generally and expressed them, on various occasions, on radio and television. The Press Council, I said, revealed a complete misunderstanding of a newspaper's duty to reveal unpalatable truths; it was doing a disservice by attempting to muzzle the Press. We were right to probe the Keeler affair, even though it was an embarrassment to the government. Even if there were sordid details it would be wrong to hide them. The British Press had a great reputation for fairness and accuracy. Of course mistakes were made, but, on the whole, it was the best in the world. I had never been told to slant an article a particular way, or to critise any individual. I have no doubt that this sometimes happens but to far less an extent than is popularly believed. I have heard stories, for example, about 'black lists', of people whose names should never be mentioned, but I've never seen one.

Whether the Press Council should be given power to deal with those who offend against a code of behaviour is an entirely different matter. We do not agree with foot-in-door journalism, nor with unwarranted intrusion into private grief. But the Press has a job to do — remember the affair of Burgess and Maclean? — and those who would like things hushed up must never be allowed to have their way.

The first thing to get clear is that a newspaper is a business. Some criticise the profit motive of the popular Press. But a newspaper without financial strength is far more vulnerable to undesirable influences. We want no one to be in a position to influence newspapers to suit his own ends. A newspaper must print the news and its views without fear. If it is financially sound, it has a great safeguard.

There is only one answer to the question: do you give the reader what he wants or what he ought to have? It is some of both. There would be a swift end to any newspaper, or Editor, who tried to cram one message after another down his readers' throats. They just wouldn't have it and the paper would be on the rocks. A popular newspaper must give people what they want, and include accurate reporting and authoritative opinion. An Editor must see his newspaper as a whole — exciting, gay, titivating, important, objective, authoritative, informative and sporting. I wouldn't attempt to put these in order.

The question of good taste is a difficult one. Few people who read popular newspapers are offended by them. I was critised for printing the life story of Jane Mansfield, a prominent young woman if there ever was one. It was absurd. Some critics of the News of the World say we are concerned only with sex and violence. It is obvious that those who say that don't read the paper. We are not afraid to look at the world as it really is. We are not afraid to report what actually goes on. We do not invent the news. We hold up a mirror to life and reflect it faithfully.

One of the Editor's great concerns is the balance of the paper. In my time an average edition contained over a hundred items of news and features. Consider some of the subjects covered in one issue taken at random: the Thalidomide babies, a heart operation on girl twins, a jungle story, a blind woman who can now see, a boom city, a couple who are strangers under the same roof, a dream house for the family, pensioners' problems, letters to the editor, books, the political situation, a spy story, the Wildlife Fund, the squire back to face fraud charges, news of the day, a competition page, the Stock Exchange and gardening. We also gave space to a secret court to which we strongly objected, and the story of a nannie and a butler. And I haven't mentioned motoring, missing persons, unclaimed money, pigeons, fishing, every kind of sport, discs, television, wedding anniversaries. One-fifth of the whole space was devoted to sport, and about one-third to advertising.

Thousands of readers are each year relieved of anxiety by our experts. We seldom let them down. It's so easy to level charges at newspapers. It's usually done by those who haven't stopped to think or haven't read them.

Sometimes we make mistakes, but the wonder is that more mistakes do not occur, having regard to the speed of production. Endless trouble is taken to avoid errors. A newspaper hates mistakes more than the readers.

We have been charged with irresponsibility, but our reporters and commentators are responsible people. We are trivial, they say. But what's wrong with a laugh and a joke? Men and women need to escape from hard work and household chores. They enjoy a joke and we're glad to be able to supply them.

Naturally, we expect the charge of sensationalism. If the news is sensational and we report it, does this mean we are a sensational newspaper? If so I accept the description. But if it means that we magnify things out of all proportion, then I absolutely deny it. The sense of the drama of life, and of the dangers and thrills and shocks experienced by ordinary people, have been the material for great dramatists throughout history.

Pornography is a favourite word of our critics, who seem to forget that the Press is strictly controlled by the laws of obscenity. No Editor wishes to run foul of the law. But we do not want to be squeamish, or to be prudish. We believe in calling a spade a spade. We believe in reporting life as it is, not as something imagined, not as something genteel and without flesh and blood.

A story that is racy, colourful and true appeals to all. It would be a poor outlook, not only for us but for the cinema and theatre, if it were not so. Newspapers do not set out deliberately to distort the news. A politically independent newspaper, like the News of the World, has no axe to grind. We print facts and comment fairly and freely. An Editor wants to sell papers. He has to. If he doesn't the paper folds up, and he gets fired. His object is to tell his readers what goes on; to interpret the news as well as to report it. He wants to amuse and inform you; and he wants to place on the breakfast table a newspaper which is attractive to look at and is part of life.

Lee Howard, formerly Editor of the Daily Mirror, said on television: 'I believe in the anonymity of Editors. I think their papers should speak for them.' I don't agree. That may have been the case before television and radio, but I believed in publicity aimed at promoting sales, and I took most opportunities to appear on television or speak on radio. I could usually forecast the questions I would be asked: they were always about sex. The critics seemed obsessed by it. I didn't want to say there was no sex in the News of the World. In the first place it wouldn't have been true, and in the second it would not have been good publicity to say so. But I wanted to put it in perspective.

A contributor in World's Press News said: 'I almost dropped my bed-time cup of cocoa the other evening when I was confronted by Stafford Somerfield wagging his finger at me from the television. With a smooth line of sales talk, he commended his paper because it had a series about Tony Armstrong Jones. Now this really is a splendid idea; Editors actually selling their papers. It introduced a touch of authenticity which the public could not fail to appreciate.'

I was as keen to sell papers as the famous editor of the Daily Express, Arthur Christiansen. He tells how he went round the streets to see that the posters were up, that the sellers all had papers. So did I. I also got in many plugs on television. I called myself a newspaper salesman. None of this cloistered anonymity for me.

I also encouraged close co-operation with other departments of the paper. In the old days the advertisement director and the Editor were often at each other's throats.

We played together; he sold space and we got the stories to make it worth-while for the advertisers to buy it. But when it came to the pinch, the Editor was the boss. If the editorial wanted space we got it, within reason, by hook or by crook. Sometimes crook.

One rule we never relaxed: we would not back up advertising if we didn't believe in the product. Cars, for example, had to be passed by our expert, and what he said went. Our woman's editor approved everything in her line that appeared. And that went for other departments. I had the final say about advertisements, and the proofs were passed by me, or for me. Is that Fleet Street practice today? I sometimes doubt it. But that was our tradition.

Co-operation between all departments inside a newspaper office is essential. The circulation department, for example, is a bread-and-butter department. They must be told when the big stories are coming, and which areas are concerned. The editorial provide the contents of the package, circulation and publishing departments sell and deliver it on time. An Editor who falls out with his printer is a fool, yet I've seen it happen. I worked closely with three printers: Fred Phillips was big and blustering, and pushed the paper through; Harold Evans was dapper, and a martinet; Stanley Strong was skilful, bald-headed and slim, and got his way by persuasion. They all did their job. The printer is the man who gets the paper away on time, and that is paramount. To be late and miss trains is a crime. He musn't push the Editor around but the Editor must bend over backwards to help him. Mind you, you can never please printers. They always demand the result of the last race before the horses are past the post.

In my ten years of editorship, I was rarely interfered with in matters of tactics until my final year when Murdoch took over. I was appointed by the board and was responsible to the board, acting through the Chairman and managing director, who, in most of my time, was the same man. It may sound boastful, but I thought I understood our policy better than most (I had been there 25 years). I maintained that, like a general in the field, I took orders concerning the grand design, but fought the battle my way. I could be sacked, but not told what to do in detail. I see no other way to run a newspaper. There can be only one man in the Editor's chair. And that's the Editor.

We took no sides in politics in my time and gave all points of view. We treated our readers as adults and didn't try to tell them how to vote. In any event they would please themselves. We said: this is the position, here are the views of the party leaders, now make up your own minds. We believed in high wages for a fair day's work; more help for people unable to look after themselves, the old, crippled, blind and mentally handicapped. Where we saw fiddling we vigorously uncovered it; we hated pompous upstarts, and got on the necks of those who didn't play straight. We weren't afraid to attack those in high places or petty local bosses. We stood for fair play all round.

We lashed the drug-takers and stood up to the police when they were wrong, but we supported law and order. We ran a campaign for better police pay. Nurses were our darlings, and we never ceased to urge better pay and conditions for them. We pressed for improved education, but we had no time for students who didn't work hard. We took a tough line over them — no work, no grant — and we believed that those who received money from the State for their education should return it when they got well-paid jobs.

We were more concerned with the victims than the criminals; we believed in capital punishment and the lash for those who raped, for those who smashed old and crippled people over the head. We made no bones about this, and our readers overwhelmingly supported us. After my time, I thought, the paper went soft on these issues.

In international affairs we did not rush to criticise Rhodesia and South Africa, recalling that they were on our side in war. We supported entry into Europe on proper terms, and maintained that Germany should for ever remain divided. There was hardly a good British cause we failed to boost, and when it came to sport we couldn't do enough to help.

I concerned myself very much about the possible effect that details of a crime — that is, the exact method — would have on the young and weak-minded. We kept these details to a minimum. Methods used in cases of suicide were rarely mentioned by us, particularly any reference to the gas-oven. The dangers of imitative crime or self-destruction were not underrated. I am always amazed at the unthinking attitude of television in this respect. While we gave the facts, those subjects dealing with brutality and violence were treated with great care. It was important to keep in mind the possible effect on our vast audience. While having a responsibility and treating serious subjects seriously, we tried not to preach.

Lord Fisher, when Archbishop of Canterbury, said an Editor is, at heart, lonely, shy and elusive; he does not court publicity for himself; he is anxious and afraid. I didn't fit into that description anywhere. I was certainly not 'lonely, shy, elusive' nor 'anxious and afraid', and although I did not court publicity, I wasn't bothered overmuch when I got it. And I got plenty.

I enjoyed my life; to me it was great. I always said, that, if I could have afforded it, I would have paid to do the job, but I didn't have to. I'd met most people who hit the headlines, from prime ministers to murderers, from the Pope to Christine Keeler. The job was exciting, stimulating and always a battle. As for being lonely, the problem was to hide somewhere where there were no telephones, and the only place for that was on board ship, and even there they'd get me on the radio. In what other job could a country boy from Barnstaple, Devon, have a life like it? I don't know of one.

My advice to youngsters seeking jobs in Fleet Street never varied. Don't become a journalist unless you feel that you must and that nothing else will do. Even then think twice. To reach the top you must be dedicated; your work must come before home, family and everything else. No sensible girl would marry a reporter, or be one. However, if your mind is made up, the best way to begin is the old-fashioned one — start at the bottom. I began by sharpening the pencils, making the tea and lumping papers around on the back of my motor-bike every Saturday for 1s. 6d. Forty years later I could still make the tea better than most. Don't become a journalist I said, but I warn you, once you smell ink you're lost.

I made a speech on these lines to my old school, and afterwards returned to London — and the sack. I had been touched by the invitation to return to Barnstaple, for it was here that I started in the local office of the Exeter Express and Echo, as an apprentice. It was here that my maternal grandfather, who could neither read nor write, dug graves in the cemetery and was worried that he'd got some mixed up. He was a wonderful man. He ran away as a boy, joined the army, was the crack shot of his regiment and played cricket for the army in India.

I saw him pull out his teeth with secateurs, march to chapel at the age of eighty, cheer on the local rugby players, encourage two youngsters to settle their differences with their fists 'like men', and give a shilling to the winner. He was a splendid gardener and worked at one time for the Chichesters on their estate near Barnstaple. One morning he was late for work so the lady of the house put her head out of the window and called: 'I do like a man in the morning John.' 'So does my wife,' said John Rivett, 'that's why I'm late.' He got the sack, as I did. It must have run in the family.

# 22 Take-over

During the time of my editorship there was fought a sordid take-over battle for the *News of the World*. It was the bloodiest in the history of Fleet Street. It left many broken lives in its wake, ended an era and made Rupert Murdoch boss of a thriving newspaper empire.

The take-over battle was brought about by the action of one man — Professor Derek Ainslie Jackson, OBE, DFC, AFC, MA, DSc, FRS, Officer of the Legion of Merit (USA), Chevalier Légion d'Honneur. He was one of the twins fathered by former Chairman of the paper, Charles Jackson. His brother died many years earlier on the ski slopes in Switzerland.

Derek became a world-famous scientist, professor of spectroscopy at Oxford, a millionaire, a gentleman-rider in the Grand National, part-owner of the paper with the largest circulation in the world, much-decorated war-hero and much-married eccentric.

In 1968 Derek Jackson, aged sixty-two, put his shares on the market and paved the way for a bitter struggle. He finished the Carrs as a newspaper family and, like Riddell before him, offered his birthright to the highest bidder.

The first I knew that all was not well with the paper was on a morning in September 1968 when Sir William Carr, the Chairman, said: 'Let's have a drink.' At the Long Bar in the Falstaff in Fleet Street, our pub — all newspapers have their own pub — he said to me: 'Derek Jackson wants to sell his shares.' I waited, and we each drew on a long scotch and water. 'The trouble is,' continued Carr, 'I haven't got that sort of money.'

He said, that, if he offered Derek more than the market

price of 28s. per ordinary voting share, the City would require him to make a similar offer to other shareholders. Derek Jackson and his family held a little less than one-third of the shares in the company, the Carrs a little more than one-third, while the other third was held by a large number of smaller shareholders. For the first time in our many years working together Carr said he felt ill. He looked ghastly. 'Keep this to yourself,' he added.

I kept my counsel, but there came another straw in the wind. Chapman-Walker, then managing director of the News of the World, and I were on our way to lunch. At the top of Whitefriars Street, by the pillar box, he suddenly took me into his confidence. He said he had noticed that options were being taken on our shares on a call basis. There was also activity in our voting shares.

We met Carr for lunch at the Savoy and Mark Chapman-Walker blurted out: 'I suppose we couldn't be the victims of a take-over bid?' Carr made no comment. I got to know more. That summer Bill and Mark had met Derek Jackson in Paris. They had regular meetings, mostly to discuss a small French television company in which we and Derek, in his own right, had an interest. Jackson invited them to meet his new wife, his sixth.

Bill Carr thought it was a purely social occasion. In his opinion, it was neither the time nor the place to discuss business matters. But at that meeting the Professor undoubtedly raised the question of breaking the trust so that he would be in a position to sell his shares. He was much concerned about death duties. Carr believed there was no hurry; he thought Derek would speak to him again at a more appropriate moment. But Mark got the message. On the way to the station, in a cab, he said to Carr: 'Derek is getting out, presumably your family will have to bid for his shares.'

Carr had always kept Derek in the picture about the company and had sent him all the documents, even though he was not a director. They were cousins. Nothing of major importance was done without consulting him, and he also had a representative on the board. Carr always invited him to all our big occasions, and Derek sometimes came over to London from Paris, where he lived, to take part.

Jackson was told that the Carr family wanted to discuss buying the shares, but he wrote to Clive Carr, Sir William's nephew, a director, saying that he had put the matter in the hands of Rothschilds, the merchant bankers, and suggested that Sir William and Clive should see them. The current market price was 28s. At the request of the Carrs, Mr Harry Sporborg, managing director of Hambros, wrote to Rothschilds making an offer at that price. Jackson later described the price as ridiculous.

Discussing the situation, Chapman-Walker said to me: 'We are now in the age of the take-over. No longer does the fact that a large number of shares are on offer mean that they command a discount. In a company like ours, with its huge asset backing, a large block of shares is at a premium. Anybody who knows the climate of opinion in the City realises that they are a springboard for a take-over.'

On the morning of 16 October 1968, Carr went to his office feeling ill. He sent for the nurse on duty, (we had a medical department) and asked for something to make him fit for the day's work. She brought two aspirins. He looked at them in scorn, exclaiming: 'What the bloody hell do you think two aspirins are going to do for me?'

What indeed? This was the first sign of a serious illness. Bill Carr went home to bed. The telephone rang: it was his friend Sir Max Aitken, then Chairman of the Beaverbrook Group. The Evening Standard had heard that Robert Maxwell, the Labour MP, head of Pergamon Press, had slammed in a bid of more than £26 million for the News of the World Organisation (the paper and its many subsidiaries). The offer put a value of 37s. 6d. on the ordinary shares and 36s. on the 'A' (non-voting) shares. Three-quarters of the price would be in Pergamon shares with a cash alternative. The rest would be accounted for by issuing 8 per cent convertible loan stock, which could be converted into ordinary shares between 1972 and 1978 at 45s.

News of the World shares flashed upwards that afternoon by 12s. 3d. to 41s. 6d., and non-voters by 9s. 1½d. to 38s. 1½d.

Carr replaced the receiver and called Hambros, He also rang Mark and Clive, his nephew, and fixed a board meeting for the next morning. He then tried to sleep, but the pain in his throat made it impossible.

I was in a nursing home being treated for blood pressure. I got into bed and a friendly Irish nursing sister said there was nothing to do, just relax. I relaxed and idly glanced at the copy of the Evening Standard she'd given me. That did it. 'Why are you putting your trousers on?' demanded the sister. 'Something I've just remembered,' I said. Within twenty minutes I was back in the office. The splash headline said: *Maxwell bids for the News of the World.* I rushed round to see Carr and put my head round his bedroom door. He looked ill. 'See you in the morning,' he said, but he didn't.

When the directors met next day at Cliveden Place, our headquarters near Sloane Square, London, Sir William lay in bed in his flat over the boardroom. His doctor said he must stay there. For the first time the board as a whole were put in the picture. It was flatly decided to reject the Pergamon bid. Sir William, from his sickroom, called it 'impudent'. We decided to await the formal offer from Maxwell who had clearly got his hands on the Jackson shares. Mark telephoned the Professor in Paris and asked for an urgent meeting, but the answer was no; everything was being handled by Rothschilds.

I returned to the office, very concerned. It seemed to me that the board had not been told everything, and that this was very much a matter between the big money interests. In my view, money wasn't the only thing at stake. Carr put it this way: 'There are three aspects to be considered — the shareholders, the Carr family trust and the employees.' I put the staff first.

Back at my desk I asked for the file on Maxwell. I wanted to know everything about him there was to know. Then I sat down and wrote a leader for the next issue of the paper, starting with a phrase used by Mr Macmillan when he had trouble within his government.

We are having a little local difficulty at the News of the World. It concerns the ownership of the paper. Mr Robert Maxwell, a Socialist MP, is trying to take it over.

Personally I don't think he will, and I, as Editor of your paper for more than eight years and a member of the editorial staff for nearly a quarter of a century, hope his bid will fail.

I do not propose to write about the financial aspect: that will be made clear by others better qualified. I write only as the man responsible for the contents of a newspaper which, for more than fifty years, has held the highest circulation in the world.

Why do I think it would not be a good thing for Mr Maxwell, formerly Jan Ludwig Hoch, to gain control of this newspaper which, I know, has your respect, loyalty and affection — a newspaper which I know is as British as roast beef and Yorkshire pudding?

First this is an independent newspaper. We do not ask Mr Wilson or Mr Heath, or anyone else, what they would like us to say. We have no political affiliations. We say what we think, regardless of party, creed or colour.

And we speak for our readers — over 16 million of them — in every walk of life, not necessarily taking the popular view. We say what we believe to be right, but the feelings, wishes and thoughts of our readers are never out of mind. You write me thousands of letters. Every one is read. By this means we keep in the closest touch. We are concerned about your difficulties and problems. We know how tough life can be. We constantly urge more aid for the elderly, the sick, the crippled, the unemployed, those who cannot help themselves. Not only through the paper. But through our world-famous John Hilton Bureau which has fought unceasingly and successfully through the years for the downtrodden and unfairly treated.

WE WANT TO GO ON DOING THIS

But above everything, we are impartial. We are not a Conservative paper. Top Conservatives have written for us. Top Socialists, too: need I mention people like the Prime Minister, Aneurin Bevan and John Freeman? Conservatives like Sir Alec Douglas-Home, Edward Heath, Reginald Maudling, even Sir Winston Churchill himself.

Liberals like Jo Grimond and Jeremy Thorpe. Everybody who is anybody has written for the News of the World.

Why has this been possible? Because we are independent; because we hold no brief for anyone; because we care. The only questions asked are: Have our correspondents something to say? Do our readers want to read what they have to say?

I, as Editor, as those before me — there have only been six of us since 1891, we don't change very often — have been able to direct this policy because of the complete backing of the Chairman of the board, now Sir William Carr, who has followed a great family tradition. Would this attitude and policy be continued by a complete stranger, as far as Fleet Street and this newspaper are concerned, a man with no newspaper experience and a Socialist MP?

Mr Maxwell has gone on record as saying if he got control he would not change the policy of the paper. But what guarantee is there of this? Mr Maxwell has also said that he would cease to be a Socialist MP if he gained control. Which must mean that his constituents, who voted him into Parliament, come second.

But is it possible for him to support the Socialists one day and become completely impartial the next? I do not

158

think so. I believe that Mr Maxwell is interested in power and money. There is nothing wrong with that, but it is not everything.

A newspaper is not a factory; a newspaper is run by people. And as far as the editorial is concerned they are a collection of individuals of skill, temperament and inspiration, free to express their own views and to do so vigorously. We are not a chicken factory with each member laying the same egg.

Mr Maxwell had also said he would not interfere with the editorial. The Editor would be free to say and do what he likes. We don't run the News of the World like that. In every sense of the word we are a family paper. The Editor has daily contact with the Chairman. We discuss our ideas; we discuss our policy. Everybody, the Chairman, the board, editorial, advertising, production, circulation, distribution, promotion, the printer (most important), knows what is happening. We discuss; we plan.

But, and this has been so for more than one hundred years, the Editor is responsible for the contents of the paper.

If he disagrees with the Chairman he says so. He has never been forced to adopt a policy, or to write an article, about something he doesn't believe in.

As I have said, a closely-knit family. Members of families sometimes disagree. There may even be rows. But we reach agreement; we are united. Would this be so under Mr Maxwell? Who knows'?

As far as my own position is concerned, I will not work with Mr Maxwell. I do not understand his views or his policy. I do not believe he is the right man to control the greatest newspaper in the world.

After a brief history of the paper and the part played by the Carrs, I concluded:

This is a British newspaper, run by British people. Let's

keep it that way. Mr Maxwell is making a bid for great power. I do not believe he is qualified to take it. Let me be realistic. Money will decide the issue. And we are getting tremendous backing. Apart from this, I appreciate all the letters you have written giving moral support. That also matters at a time like this. Money is important though it isn't everything. We all need it but I and my colleagues also believe we are doing something worthwhile.

*We believe in this paper. We believe in you, our 16 million readers. With your support we shall win — and continue to serve you.*

All hell broke out, particularly over the phrase: 'The News of the World is as British as roast beef and Yorkshire pudding.' A good phrase I thought then, and still do. Bernard Levin really let his hair down about it. He said I had 'sobbed and gurgled' about the greatness of my paper. He called it compost with a couple of exceptionally fragrant weeds. Rancid and smearing were other epithets. My behaviour, he said, was something less than admirably British. Closer to my heart than roast beef and Yorkshire pudding were rape, indecent assault, incest, buggery and the disarrangement of young ladies' underclothing in darkened railway carriages.

A long list and not accurate. Closer to my heart was the well-being of the paper and my staff. Besides that, I do not recall reporting incest, ever, and buggery very rarely. Mr Levin had not grasped the true situation.

The Observer was kinder. They just said my leader spluttered with xenophobia! The paper, they said, was ripe for reform, was archaic and used music-hall type. That wasn't true either. One thing was certain — we had a hell of a sight more readers than the Observer. David Steel, MP, wrote in the Guardian: 'What a revolting piece of chauvinism. Mr Maxwell is not everybody's cup of tea and he knows it, but he is as disgustingly British as anybody I know. He even has a Rolls-Royce with a telephone in it. ...

Sir William Carr and members of his family who fought against the take-over bid by Robert Maxwell. STANDING: Mrs John Blyth (niece), Mr Sebastian Peake, Mr Neil Forsyth (Lady Carris brother), Miss Sarah Carr (daughter), Mr Clive Carr (nephew), Mrs Clive Carr, Mrs Rusden, Mr Peter Rusden (nephew). SEATED: Mrs William Carr (daughter-in-law), Betty, Lady Waleran (sister), Mr William Carr (son), Mrs Joan Bailey (niece), Mrs James Armstrong (mother of Mr Clive Carr), Sir William and Lady Carr, Mr James Armstrong (stepfather of Mr Clive Carr), Miss Ruth Gilmore (cousin), Mr Richard Carr (nephew) and Mrs Mattie Worthington (cousin). *(Press Association Photo).*

Sir William Carr (left) and Rupert Murdoch. (*Press Association Photo*).

Good luck, Bob'.

What these characters didn't seem to realise was that I was fighting for our newspaper. I was at war, and, when at war, I saw no point in throwing friendly leaflets. We'd learnt that in 1939. The Observer declared that our reputation for salacious reporting was fading, the paper was run on a shoe-string, with only four general reporters. (If there were only four general reporters, who were those other chaps for whom I was signing expenses sheets?) I was described as 'one of the old school, bow-tied, exuberant in manner with a big, round Charles Laughton-ish face. I pursued blimpishness and salacious puritanism with missionary zeal.' Some puritan, some missionary!

There was further uproar because I said on television that I wouldn't work for Maxwell 'for all the tea in China'.

All the papers, with the exception of our friends at the Express, seemed to be against us. I recalled Randolph Churchill's words: 'They say dog don't eat dog but it seems son of a bitch eats son of a bitch.'

Maxwell and I met on television, and it was a knockabout affair. He called me a huckster. I didn't tell him what I thought he was. He said I could remain as Editor and would not be interfered with. Carr would be offered the life presidency. 'You,' I said, 'are not going to offer anyone anything.' And I wasn't wrong.

Of our television performance, Virginia Ironside wrote in the Daily Mail: 'Maxwell, smooth, suave and unruffled, played his role of sweet reason to the hilt; the editor pleaded passionately the human side of the story, oozing as much emotion as Maxwell oozed cold business sense.'

Was it business sense? That was the question.

# 23  Round by Round

This is what our files on Robert Maxwell disclosed. He was born in Czechoslovakia, Jan Ludwig Hoch, 10 June 1923, son of a farm labourer. He joined the Resistance during the Occupation and escaped to Britain in 1940, without a penny and with little or no education. He spoke no English when he arrived in Liverpool, aged sixteen, but now speaks it perfectly, plus seven other languages. He had had several names, but there was nothing in this to his discredit, in fact the reverse. There were good reasons for the changes in name; it was frequently done when men and women from Occupied countries went back to fight the Nazis as he had done. Maxwell joined the British Army, and was decorated with the MC on the battlefield by Field-Marshal Montgomery and commissioned. He reached the rank of captain.

He had made rapid progress after the war, joining the Foreign Office German Section and, at twenty-three, had become the British Press Officer responsible for controlling the new German-language newspapers.

In 1947 he set up as a bookseller and later founded Robert Maxwell and Company. Sir Charles Hambro thought so highly of him he gave him a credit of £25,000. Maxwell changed the name of his company to Pergamon Press. He was one of the first publishers in Britain to see the advantages of specialising in scientific and technical books and journals. Maxwell himself said that, a year after receiving the Hambros credit, he borrowed a million and paid it back in six years.

He extended Pergamon by acquiring more companies and, in 1967, widened his interests still further by combining with the British Printing Corporation in launching International Learning Systems Corporation. He published Chambers Encyclopaedia and several other major books of reference. His progress with scientific publications was revealed by these figures: 1961: 90 journals and 213 new book titles; 1965: 120 and 600. Those figures were to be further increased.

Additional notes revealed that he had taken over Simkin Marshall, the book wholesalers, in 1951, but they failed three years later. He bought Caxton Publishing in 1967, and the printing works from the Co-operative Press in 1968.

Pergamon was floated in July 1964 at 17s. 6d. per share, putting a value on the company of £3·5 million. Maxwell and his family trusts sold £1·1 million in shares, or 29 per cent of the equity. The shares doubled eighteen months later, and they sold a further £1·1 million. In 1966 Maxwell bought George Newnes subscription books from IPC for £1 million. In 1967 the Pergamon stock market valuation was £12·7 million. In 1968 Maxwell and his family interests owned 34 per cent of Pergamon, and the profit forecast for the year 1969 was £2·5 million.

Maxwell was described as a tall, dark, good-looking man, bold in manner, with a fondness for electric blue suits and gaudy ties. His wife, Elizabeth, was French and they had eight children. He lived in style at Headington Hill Hall, Oxford, and had a West End flat. His Rolls-Royce was on the telephone and he had been summoned for shaving while driving. He had produced films, written books, played chess and enjoyed mountain-climbing.

He was Labour MP for Buckingham, but said he would retire if he got the News of the World. He had once declared to the voters, 'I am one of you', and had run a 'Back Britain' campaign with enthusiasm.

All this made Bob Maxwell a formidable opponent, and his meteoric rise was greatly to his credit. I made enquiries to find out what they thought of him in the publishing business. Here were some of the quotes that came up:

'Highly competent business man who can squeeze more profit out of assets than anyone else.' 'Brash, abrasive, ambitious, energetic and talkative.' In the House of Commons Harold Wilson put him in charge of the kitchens, which he managed very well.

I also studied some of the things he was reported to have said: 'I chose Britain; I like Britain. You were lucky enough to be born in it ... I am not interested in money as a means to power and I only want power in order to do things ... I am regarded with envy ... I'm just a chap who's interested in communications and making the printing industry more efficient ... I try to help other people and my country ... I'm just a chap who wants to stop Britain sliding ... I am not a fellow who toes the line ... I can't get on with men ... The establishment is out to get me.'

The Sunday Times described him as 'a brash, but charming operator, supremely patriotic, efficient and effective'. Maxwell was no doubt all those things, but was he claiming too much for Pergamon? He had to justify their forecast of vast profits of £2·5 million in 1969. We wanted to know more.

Maxwell wouldn't appear with me on television a second time because, he said, I had made a personal attack on him. To me that had only been the opening salvo and I was surprised that he had ducked.

My notes of October 1968 reveal that our directors were now meeting daily. This is how the battle went, round by round.

*18 October*   The two sides are drawn up like this: Pergamon have the promise of the Jackson family's 25 per cent of the voting shares. The Carrs and their supporters have 27 per cent. About 3,500 private individuals hold the balance. The total is 9,600,000 shares. My bet is that the majority will stick with us, no matter what the offer is. Our shares at 48s. 6d. today, 11s. up on bid.

*19 October*   Shares go to 49s., 11s. 6d. above Maxwell's first offer. Maxwell now said to be in the market. He's bought

50,000. Myer's, our stockbrokers, have bought 60,000 shares 'for clients'. I hear that a secret group have come in on our side. Both sides are buying all the shares they can. The sides stand today: Maxwell 25 per cent, Carrs and friends 30 per cent.

*20 October*   Carr said to me today: 'Remember you've got a newspaper to look after.' I remembered. According to the Observer, Derek Jackson said: 'I told Sir William nine months ago I wanted to sell. He should accept Maxwell's offer.'

*21 October*   We're certain now Maxwell will increase his bid. Voters at 49s. 6d. today, non-voters down to 39s. Maxwell says the Carrs are cracking. Says he's got 30 per cent. But the Carrs show no sign of cracking. UK Press Gazette is right on our side. Nobody in The Street, they say, wants to see Maxwell win. Good for them. Bit of a change from the other papers.

*22 October*   Maxwell's new offer is £34 million. This values the voters at 50s. against the first bid of 37s. 6d., non-voters 42s. 9d. against 36s. Maxwell says this is his final offer. There is talk about the City Code and 'the possibility', says The Times, 'of a sizeable minority of our shareholders being locked out'. Now revealed that thousands of shares have changed hands: 300,000 for us; 50,000 for Pergamon; price down to 46s.

*23 October*   By our count we now have over 40 per cent. The actual terms of Pergamon's new offer are three of its ordinary shares and 48s. of 8 per cent Convertible Unsecured Loan Stock for every four News of the World ordinaries, and three shares and 24s. of stock for every four non-voters. The Telegraph is dead-set against us for some reason. Today they call on us to 'come clean'.

*24 October*   The papers have 'gone a bundle' on a picture of the united Carr family. Maxwell will have to look hard for the cracks he talks about. Shares now 47s. Patrick Sergeant of the Daily Mail says: 'The battle is coming to the crunch. We do not want another scandal and more pressure for outside rule of the City ...' Sergeant reminds the directors that we should not have regard for our jobs, for our feelings about the newspaper, or for personal or family shareholdings. I hear a whisper that we might be getting an important ally. Everyone is 'keeping mum' and it's all very secret.

My telephone rings at midnight. It's an old friend on the night desk at the Express: 'Your saviour is here,' he says. 'It's young Rupert Murdoch from Australia. We're splashing it in the morning.' The Express do it big. Their headlines scream: 'Midnight: Australian in big share deal. Maxwell loses newspaper bid'. A bit previous, but I believe it's right.

Bill Carr filled in the details for me. 'Sporborg of Hambros pressed on me the need for an ally,' he said. 'Had I refused, Hambros might have withdrawn and we should have been in the soup. Sporborg told me that Murdoch was in London, but he didn't want me to go to meet him, either because I was Chairman or, maybe, because I was not very well — maybe because I was too old. Dinner was suggested. I said that, on the family side — this was a family matter because it really goes back in history to the Carrs versus the Jacksons — I was quite certain that my nephew, Clive, should be present and my son, William, to represent our family's large shareholding. To this Harry Sporborg said "Excellent," and they all went out and had dinner.

'Next day, I heard that reactions were favourable and I was asked to meet Murdoch the following morning. He would come to breakfast. Normally I do not have breakfast on the third floor of Cliveden Place. But on this occasion Mrs Holmes, the housekeeper, cooked us scrambled eggs there. She must have put milk in them; they were awful. Nobody ate breakfast. Mind you, they had not come to eat breakfast. The facts were quite clear; Murdoch was interested, and Clive and William had given him the once-over, and were satisfied that he was an honourable man and one with whom we could work.

'Murdoch made one condition on which I was prepared to give in. He said that, naturally, I would want to continue as Chairman and he would want to be joint managing director. I saw nothing wrong with that. He was a young man who had obviously made a success of his business.

'I told him that he must not overlook that I had a contract that would run until I was sixty-five in seven years' time. "Oh," said Murdoch. "Sporborg had said there was no reason why the contract should be disturbed." If I was prepared to be consultant and Chairman, everything could remain as it was and Murdoch would take over the running operations. I was not in a strong position and I agreed.'

What became clear to me was that, when the chips are down, in these situations only money talks. The other directors, myself included, were mere ciphers.

# 24  Our Ally

On 24 October 1968 at 2.30 pm, the Stock Exchange suspended dealings in our shares. There was no reflection on either party, they said, but shareholders should be given a chance to make up their minds on Maxwell's offer and the merits of the company's defence.

I now wanted to know all about Rupert Murdoch. It was reported that he was thirty-seven, dynamic and ambitious, and had already bought, through his bankers, Morgan Grenfell, about 3½ per cent in our group. He was the head of an Australian newspaper chain valued at £20 million on the Sydney Stock Exchange. He had been at Oxford and, while there, was on the committee of the Labour Club.

The son of an Australian newspaper owner, Sir Keith Murdoch, he was left a small share in a modest Adelaide newspaper when his father died in 1952, and had steamed ahead. Soon he was buying up other papers, moving into radio, television and records. He had multiplied his company's profits of £30,000 ten times by 1960.

He was a great out-of-doors man, it was said, fond of riding, yachting, flying his own plane. He was twice married. There were two accounts about Murdoch's attitude to his staff: first that he was a great sacker, and second that he inspired great loyalty.

One story about him caused me to smile. He was reported to have 'ticked off' an editor for wearing suede shoes in the office, exploding: 'What are you running — a newspaper or a bloody jazz band?' I didn't think I would stop wearing suede shoes. When I first met him at our headquarters, I noted his easy laugh, friendly smile, dark brown hair and plump figure. His Australian accent was ghastly. I was told he could be tough, but was fair, worked hard, and expected others to do the same. He came to my London flat for a drink, and brought with him his pretty young wife and a new baby in a basket. He carried it and we thought it charming. Lady Carr thought he needed a little polishing, and maybe that was true, for he proved as hard as a diamond.

On 24 October our shares were up to 50s. 6d. Hambros got another 244,000 before dealings were suspended, and their target of one million had been reached.

Next I heard how Murdoch had dashed to England. He had walked into the Sydney office of his News Ltd to find an urgent cable from London telling him of Maxwell's bid. He immediately cabled his friend Lord Catto of Morgan Grenfell, asking him to contact our bankers, Hambros, and make a preliminary sounding. Next, he instructed his London office to give him full details about the bid.

Events moved fast. In London Catto saw Sporborg, who told Carr of Murdoch's interest. Then Catto telephoned Murdoch and advised him to be ready to fly to England at short notice. But, for the moment, the heat was off and Murdoch thought it safe to keep an appointment 500 miles away in Melbourne.

While Murdoch was in the air, Catto called again. The situation in London had changed. Maxwell was about to increase his offer. Murdoch had better come at once. The staff of News Ltd were alerted to contact Murdoch as soon as he landed. They did, and he got into another plane to return immediately to Sydney, sending a message to his wife to meet him at the airport with a suitcase and his passport.

They held the Sydney-London plane. Everything clicked into place, and Murdoch spent the next thirty hours at 30,000 feet, studying his brief. In London, Catto was waiting and took him off to his country house to put him further in the picture. They sat down in their hideout to work out a plan, and it was a clever one.

At the Savoy, Murdoch told reporters he would inject

part of his group into the News of the World in exchange for shares. He would give us a spread outside the United Kingdom and put it into a large, profitable business in Australia. The details had not been worked out. He had already bought a $3\frac{1}{2}$ per cent interest in our voting shares and had been prepared to buy 9 per cent. But the City Takeover Panel had said 'stop'. He now required the shareholders' approval, and a nod from both the Bank of England and the Reserve Bank of Australia. He would become our joint managing director with Sir William Carr, who would continue as Chairman.

What was clear now was that, if Murdoch succeeded, he would have got our organisation very cheaply. Mark Chapman-Walker put it this way: it was one of the boldest intrusions into Fleet Street that had ever taken place.

Of Murdoch it must be said that, like a good newspaperman, he'd got cracking when the story broke. He flew where the action was taking place and got his scoop. Others had sat back.

This was the position on 26 October: the Carrs and their friends had 40 per cent of the 9,600,000 shares; Maxwell the second biggest lot — 25 per cent; Murdoch $3\frac{1}{2}$ per cent. The Australian's plan was now revealed. We were to create thousands more shares, and he was to get them in return for Australian assets. 'A small bait to catch a big whale,' said Maxwell.

My notes for 26 October read:

Two statements made by us that we and our associates have more than half the voting shares, Maxwell denies it and fights on, and by Murdoch that under the new arrangements News Ltd will get 40 per cent of the voting shares, including the new ones, making him the dominant partner. What a coup!

We come out with a statement that association with Pergamon would not be in the best interest of our shareholders, and we give all the reasons we can think of for saying so. In a few words: it would not work. Pergamon has no experience of a big newspaper, we said. Our profits were increasing; we were on the upward curve; and our asset value was very considerable.

Patrick Sergeant of the Mail says our deal with Murdoch is a blatant example of a forestalling action and a denial of shareholders' rights. In the City they are saying that a coach and horses has been driven through the Takeover Code.

*27 October* Murdoch claims that he and Carr together have 51 per cent of the shares. He denies he is anti-British; he's pro-Australian. He's asked a question which particularly interests me: would he change the character of the paper? 'Only after a long, hard look,' was the reply. I smell a fight.

Inevitably questions are to be asked in the House. Mr Arthur Lewis wants to know what's happening and gets a guarded reply from Mr Diamond, Chief Financial Secretary. Obviously he hasn't a clue. Catto is bullish. Asked why shareholders should accept the arrangements with Murdoch and not 50s. a share from Pergamon, he replies: 'Mr Murdoch will be able to make the shares worth far more.'

Criticism of the City Panel is growing. The Economist says it will be a dead duck unless it exerts itself. The Times declares confidence in the Panel has been undermined. Maxwell is off to see the Panel again shouting: 'It's not fair.' I don't fancy it's getting him anywhere.

*27 October* Can this be true? The Professor has been in London to see the Panel. He kept out of our way. He's saying that Hambros offered him 28s. on 3 October, and now say 50s. isn't good enough. He's said to be hopping mad.

The Sunday Times headline today: 'Can the whiz-kid make it?' They mean Murdoch. 'Bigamy in Bouverie Street,' says the Observer. Not unamusing.

*28 October* Maxwell is still shouting it's unfair and has gone to see the Panel yet again. Scream as he likes, the deal is in the Kangaroo's pouch. Maxwell's complaint is that by buying in the market, Hambros and Morgan Grenfell have frustrated a bona fide offer. Sporborg snaps his fingers at that.

Says Murdoch: 'I like Sir William as a decent and honourable man. It's only human for him to want to stay in the centre of his own newspaper.' [Later we shall see what happened.]

*29 October*  Everybody has been off to see the Panel today; everybody is protesting. They must know Sporborg's done them in the eye. A charming man, grey-haired Harry Sporborg with an inscrutable smile and drooping eye, he's as clever as a bag of monkeys. He's got our Stock Exchange quote restored.

Anthony Crosland, President of the Board of Trade, says: 'As there are very few sanctions at the Panel's disposal, it will have to rely mainly on the respect shown for its views.' Forgive me for laughing. There's no respect for anything in this jungle warfare.

*30 October*  Announced that the Takeover Code has not been breached. Sir Humphrey Mynors, the Chairman of it, says so. Just bent a bit, presumably.

It is inevitable that a Sunday newspaper comes up with the headline: 'Rape of the News of the World.' 'Maxwell's New World' was another headline. One correspondent has likened Bill Carr's position to Churchill's during the war, when Britain took Russia as an ally. We were on the same side only because there was a common enemy.

Says the Express: 'If things are allowed to stand as they are Murdoch will end up in control.' I give points to them for their headline: 'Paper dreams of the Bustling Bookman.' Other papers, keen on the human angle, think up: 'I love children, says the Socialist Millionaire.' ' "We chose to be British," says Mrs Maxwell.' ' "No sin in making money," says Mr Maxwell.' The Times calls him: 'Maxwell, Soldier of Fortune.'

I now know that Murdoch has written to Carr saying that, as soon as the purchase and share issues takes place, Carr would retire as managing director on suitable terms and that Murdoch would then become sole managing director. [Earlier it was to have been joint managing director.] But Murdoch said he would support the continuation of a member of the Carr family as chairman, and he hoped Sir William would continue in that capacity. He looked forward to working with him and his colleagues for many years. [A very interesting statement as events will prove.]

*31 October* A joint statement by the President of the Board of Trade and the Governor of the Bank of England says the possible reinforcement of new take-over controls by the Board of Trade have been discussed, also the radical reorganisation of the Panel. The City believes there is likely to be a full-time chairman, more permanent staff, redrafting of the Code and sanctions for code-breakers.

*2 November* The Panel announces again that no one has broken the City Code. But Hambros (for us), Hill Samuel (for Pergamon) and Morgan Grenfell (for Murdoch) have given undertakings that votes attaching to shares, acquired since the original announcement, will not be exercised. That means we are back to square one, with the Carrs holding over 30 per cent, and, in Maxwell's hand, Jackson's 25 per cent. All important are the votes of the little people in the middle. 'Fair enough,' says Maxwell, but I don't believe he understands the situation. The little people will be on our side, there's no doubt about that.

Newspaper views about the Panel's verdict are not complimentary; they range from 'Whiter than White' to 'The code is dead — long live the code!' A new, tougher code is promised for the future. But the stable door was open and the horse gone.

*6 November* Lord Francis Williams takes a dig at us today. He calls me 'True-blue Somerfield' and says that it may shock me to hear that Murdoch has Labour leanings. I bet my Liberal record is longer.

The Times declares that a victory for Carr is not certain. That gives me more hope that the opposite is true. The

House of Commons are now having their say. A Labour MP wants to know what action the President of the Board of Trade is going to take. Crosland says: 'No action is being taken. But recent events have given rise to acute anxiety and disquiet.' He had a responsibility to small shareholders, especially those who did not have merchant banks to advise them. 'The Government will act if the code fails to operate satisfactorily.' I doubt it.

*9 November* One city Editor has called for Ten Commandments in place of the City Code but does not suggest any. Why not 'Thou shalt not covet'.

*11 November* Wilson speaks: 'The Government may be forced to interfere if the City does not enforce its own discipline. Recent events have cast a shadow over the workings of some of our institutions. Shareholders' rights must be upheld, but it is for the City to act to preserve their own good name.' It's all so much hot air. Wilson declares that the bulk of the City's institutions act honourably, but there is a minority concerned, not with earning, only with making money. He's got something there.

*4 November* Here comes Murdoch, back from Australia, smiling and fatter; beautiful blonde wife on one arm and baby on the other. This boy doesn't miss a trick. Everyone will fall for the baby. Let battle commence. Murdoch declares he's got complaints to make to the Stock Exchange Council and the Takeover Panel. Maxwell's reply is to sue in Australia for £466,000 over an article about the doorstep sale of books. I thought it was about time for the writs to fly. One thing is for sure, we're not frightened of writs at 30 Bouverie Street. I've always said: 'Come early and avoid the rush.'

*9 December* Seconds out, round 14 of the great 15-round contest. We declare that next year we expect profits of £4·5 million after tax. I hope it comes off. Says the Daily Telegraph: 'This expression of hope and confidence does not, in view of the company's past record, carry much conviction.' But the Guardian describes it as a good straight left, but not a knock-out. The Times says our package is a perfectly acceptable defensive move and it will make Maxwell's task much harder.

*16 December* Carr writes to our shareholders, giving full details of our proposals. We shall increase our capital by 5,100,000 shares, which will be allotted to News Ltd. Murdoch will become managing director, as he would represent the largest shareholding, and he will put six directors on the board out of a total of sixteen. There follows a list of magazines and other Australian interests being acquired. My friends in The Street chip me about them. Am I booked as Editor of the *Dandenong Journal*, *Best Bets* or *Surfers' Paradise*? I plump for Paradise.

The Evening Standard announces: 'The News of the World directors sued for conspiracy.' It looks like a last throw. Some of my colleagues are worried; they are not accustomed to writs. Bringing proceedings against us are the Public Trustee, the Jacksons and others, including Nathaniel Charles Jacob Rothschild. They are claiming damages for alleged breach of fiduciary obligations and injurious falsehood.

Hambros and News Ltd are joined with us. The writ seeks an injunction to restrain shares, bought by Hambros since 16 October, being voted at the extraordinary general meeting. Knowing a little about the courts and how they work, I have abjured my colleagues to be of good cheer; nothing will come of it and only the lawyers will benefit.

It was all put in perspective for me by Lord Goodman, one of the cleverest lawyers in London, when I met him in the lift at the office. I asked him what was happening about the action. 'My dear Somerfield,' he said, 'this is an action, the cessation of which would be a matter of some concern to the solicitors.' And I chortled all the way to my room and wrote the words down. They were too Goodman to miss. [As a joke, I hope, Murdoch said to me after he met Goodman for the first time: 'Great chap that, we must get him to break your contract.' 'Too late,' I replied, 'he drafted

175

it.' It was not quite true, but he had written a letter about it and did not charge me a penny.]

*22 December*   'The choice should be Maxwell.' Who says so? Why, the Sunday Telegraph, our friends. The barrage of abuse, it says, has descended to levels almost worthy of the News of the World columns. Cries the Observer: 'The likely outcome is something about which, under more normal circumstances, the News of the World would be seething with righteous indignation.' They just don't know how much we are seething.

*30 December*   The last fling of this bad old year. I rush up to the High Court to hear an application for an *ex parte* injunction to restrain the trustees of our pension fund from using the fund's 600,000 ordinary shares in our favour. The Judge isn't going to wear that one. He can see the hand behind it.

*1 January*   In the High Court this morning Mr Justice Megarry refuses to grant an injunction, and tells the pensioners, pure simple souls, that they have been used as pawns in the fight for control of a newspaper. That's just it. And it's moving to a climax. Happy New Year? I wonder.

# 25 Confrontation

2 January 1969 and all is lined up for the special general meeting of shareholders at the Connaught Rooms, London. Mark Chapman-Walker and I have written and rewritten the Chairman's speech till he is satisfied with it. We've cut it to the bone but I've got in a sentence I know will bring the cheers: 'I shall remain as your Chairman, a position held by my father and my grandfather before me.' As I came in I saw Bill, looking white and ill. He should be in bed. My goodness, he's brave. He's had one injection already.

All the Carrs are here, the ladies dressed as though for church in their fur coats and hats. In the conference room the television lights are blazing. A reporter grabs me by the arm: 'How's it going?' 'Not to worry,' I say, 'we've won.' Who are we? I wonder.

I take my seat on the left of the long directors' green baize table. I guess there are five hundred people here, and one feels a bit foolish perched up as though on a stage.

There's Maxwell down in the hall in a light blue suit and wearing an Astrakhan hat. He must take it off. He does. He looks swarthy and grim. Does he know he has lost the battle? And there's Murdoch in the centre, smiling; if he's nervous he doesn't show it. Lady Carr, looking very gay and wearing her brightest face, smiles and I raise a hand.

It's 11.30, and in comes Bill to a burst of applause. It lasts forty-eight seconds by my watch. Naturally the microphone doesn't work at first. Bill begins on a subdued note. I look at hundreds of pink, upturned faces through the haze of tobacco smoke. Some I recognise as our staff, who had been lent shares so they could attend. Afterwards they were required to return them.

177

'Thank you for your attendance,' says Bill, stumbling over the script. 'It's the best-attended meeting in the history of the company.' That gets a laugh. But there is silence when he outlines his reasons for the meeting in simple, straightforward terms. The struggle for control of the company had begun when Professor Jackson and his family, holding 25 per cent of the voting shares, intimated their wish to sell. This led to the Pergamon bid, but the News of the World decided, after obtaining professional advice, that such a merger had no commercial logic. Did they, or did they not, approve a resolution which would enable the News of the World to carry into effect the proposed transaction with News Ltd? That was the question.

'Pergamon has no experience of newspapers,' says Carr almost in a whisper, 'and the unions regard their proposals with dismay.' Applause from the floor from our chaps. 'We have no faith in Pergamon shares.' continues Bill, his voice gaining strength. He takes a sip of water. There is dead silence. There is scorn in his voice now: 'Pergamon say that our profit forecasts are highly suspect. My forecasts over the years have been borne out by events. I am deeply confident today. We are not rushing into the arms of News Ltd as suggested. Linking-up represents a unique opportunity to establish a major stake in a fast-growing, fast-developing country. Mr Murdoch has enjoyed great success in Australia and he will bring new blood and energy to our organisation.'

Bill sits down to great applause. He looks worn-out. He calls on Murdoch.

Murdoch rises from the centre of the hall in the front row. His dark clothes, tie and white shirt are discreet. He has an engaging smile. He looks fresh — boyish almost. Once again I think how excruciating is his Australian accent. He was laying his reputation on the line, he said.

The assets of News Ltd, he told us, were first-class. That is why the News of the World board selected them. The linking of the two organisations made sense and had great possibilities. He then paid tribute to Sir William, and said how glad he was that he would be remaining as Chairman. (Cheers for that.) The speech, well put across, lasted three minutes — just right.

Now for questions. Bill shuffles his papers. He's got the answers ready. We saw to that. Maxwell rises, but another shareholder gets in first: 'What's your name and what are your qualifications to speak?' Maxwell takes it calmly: 'Robert Maxwell and I represent 20,000 shares.'

That starts it. There is a hiss and a boo and shouts of 'sit down'. Maxwell stands his ground. Sir William holds up his hand for silence and it comes immediately.

Maxwell asks politely: 'May I make a statement in reply to your opening remarks?' 'Yes,' answers Sir William, 'but you must not speak longer than Mr Murdoch. That was three minutes, ten seconds.' A shout of laughter. That nettles Maxwell. He stabs a finger at Sir William: 'Are you going to give me a fair hearing, or not?' More booing: it's getting rough. 'I challenge you,' Maxwell says to the Chairman amid more booing, 'to deny that Hambros and News attempted to gain control of 51 per cent of the votes of the company before the meeting.' Carr looks shocked. 'Of course I contest that,' he replies.

Maxwell says: 'I see you've got the spontaneous answers to questions ready.' Cries of 'Withdraw'. 'Get on with your speech,' advises the Chairman. Maxwell gets on. News of the World profits had only moved in one direction — downwards. It was a lamentable indictment of the board. Pergamon's record was so much better. 'The News of the World's actions might be all right in the USSR and East Germany,' he says. The rest of the sentence was drowned in angry shouts of 'Go home,' 'Get back to the Old Vic', 'Get lost'.

Maxwell, practised politician, waited for the shouts to subside. Then he challenged Sporborg: 'You not only offered to buy 750,000 shares from Jackson at 28s., but suggested he might wish to sell the remainder of his holdings at prices 1s. under the market price. I challenge you to deny it.' Snapped Sporborg: 'I do deny it.' Maxwell clearly was not going to ruffle him. Bankers don't seem to ruffle easily!

Sir William stepped in now, reminding Maxwell that his time was up. In fact he'd had more than his share. But Maxwell continued: 'Why had Sir William said some unions would regard the Pergamon take-over with apprehension? There were no facts to support it. Why had Hambros said 28s. a share was fair and generous, and thirteen days later described the Pergamon bid of 48s. unreasonable?' But he had lost the interest of the meeting; the shareholders were getting bored.

Sir William stepped in again with the house on his side: 'I am tired of listening to a great number of half-truths from Mr Maxwell.' 'He's out of order,' someone yells. 'I seek the protection of the chair,' says Maxwell, and gets a derisive laugh. The Chairman signals for quiet. 'I'll give you another minute,' he says.

Maxwell turns his back and addresses himself to 'uncommitted shareholders'. 'If you accept the Pergamon offer you will get 52s. for an ordinary share and 42s. a non-voting share ...' A voice: 'In cash?' Maxwell ignores that question. All the News of the World could do, he continued, was to ask Murdoch to rescue them. If shareholders supported the News of the World they would be voting for a substantial fall in the market price of their investment ... Pergamon had an outstanding record ...

Sir William rose wearily: 'I don't think the shareholders care a "twopenny cuss" what you think about their board,' he said. 'Did the meeting wish to hear any more from Mr Maxwell?' Cries of No! No! Maxwell pressed the point about Pergamon's cash offer. Carr replied: 'What is money when you can get so much more out of life?' An unusual remark for a company chairman to make to shareholders. But astonishingly, it got a murmur of sympathetic support.

'I must now put the resolution to the meeting,' he said.

'Do the shareholders approve of the link-up between the News of the World Organisation and News Ltd of Australia, which increases the company's capital to £6,573,000 by making a further 5,100,000 ordinary shares of 5s. each, to be allotted as fully-paid to News Ltd, and increases the maximum number of directors from ten to sixteen?'

On a show of hands: for 299, against 20.

Sir William then said because of the importance of the matter he demanded a poll. Everyone seemed to get out of the hall at once, except for Carr, Murdoch, Maxwell and the rest of the board. I congratulated Bill, who sat in a chair in the ante-room, surrounded by his family, advisers and friends. He looked ghastly. I pressed his arm and he gave me a thin smile. That's the end for you, old boy, I thought.

The poll result was: for 4,526,822, against 3,246,937.

The result convinced me that we could have won the battle alone, but it was also clear that Murdoch was now the boss.

Maxwell declared: 'The law of the jungle has prevailed.' Presumably the law of the jungle is the survival of the fittest. Carr and Murdoch clasped hands for the photographers, with Harry Sporborg smiling into the camera. I went in search of a large drink.

From atop a horse in the Swiss Alps Jackson declared: 'I am the most disappointed man in the whole world. I regard the News of the World board as raving mad. I still want to sell my shares.' Later he did so.

Two years later, Price Waterhouse, the City accountants, and Sir Henry d'Avigdor Goldsmidt, made separate reports on Maxwell's Pergamon; and the Financial Times commented that, if the Carr family had got a hint of the situation now presented, they would never have needed to call in Mr Rupert Murdoch as their saviour. The News of the World would still have been run by the Carrs.

On 20 October 1970 the action against the News of the World directors was dismissed and all the charges and allegations were withdrawn; on the 17 February 1972 the revised City Panel came into force, with Lord Shawcross as Chairman and with a full-time director-general. The duty of the Panel, they said, was the enforcement of good business standards, not the enforcement of law. Perhaps all had not been in vain, at least in this regard.

# 26 Disenchantment

Before the annual meeting of 2 January 1969 Rupert Murdoch said to Bill Carr: 'Will you come round to my flat with Lady Carr afterwards?' He was staying at that time in a flat on London's Embankment. 'We will drink in sorrow if we lose; if we win we will celebrate.'

'My wife was "absolutely barking," said Carr to me. ' "What the bloody hell do you mean by agreeing to go to a party? You should be in bed".' Replied Bill: 'I shall have to put in an appearance. After tonight you can do what you like with my sick body. But tonight I shall go to the party.'

He went and sat next to Sir Max Aitken. I saw him there, looking grim and unhappy. We had a brief word. In severe pain, he stayed for only fifteen minutes. The following day he was 'carted off to hospital and chopped up', as he put it.

He never returned to Bouverie Street, except for one meeting of the trustees of the pension fund in May 1970. He was operated on at St Mary's, Paddington, and when I visited him there he was very ill and weak. But one piece of news was comforting.

We had feared cancer but, in Bill's words, 'they took a slice of my spine and it showed no sign of it, there was no malignancy, but I had a large aneurism [a widening or dilation of an artery]. Fortunately it did not break.'

But there would have to be another operation.

Carr returned to his country house at Bentley Wood, Halland in Sussex, to gain strength. The pain persisted, and in April he was back in St Mary's. Mr Eastcott operated. By putting a tube down the aorta, the main artery, he took out the aneurism. While Carr was recovering in hospital Murdoch went to see him. Carr understood him to say he had made an offer to buy a million of Jackson's shares at 40s. each, but had no intention of gaining 51 per cent of the company, giving him complete control. Jackson's remaining shares had been, or were being, placed.

So the Professor hadn't done so badly. His shares had been used by Maxwell to fight Carr, and, Maxwell beaten, he had made a deal with Murdoch, collecting a couple of millions, with more to come.

In March Murdoch thought it necessary to write to Carr, who was still in hospital, saying that the company could only have one executive boss. As Managing Director, and in control of a virtual majority of the voting shares, that person had to be him. He, and he alone, would be responsible to the board for the management and results of all the company's activities. The letter concluded by saying that Murdoch would pay Carr all the respect and attention due to him as Chairman, but that Carr should avoid confusion by resigning from subsidiary companies.

Carr, alone in his hospital room, was an unhappy man. 'He wants me to be a nonentity,' he said to me. His health improved slowly and he returned to his Sussex home to convalesce. In June, Murdoch drove down from London to see him. 'I thought, perhaps, he wanted to pay a courtesy call and wish me well,' said Carr.

But Murdoch had something else on his mind and he came quickly to the point. He wanted Carr's resignation as Chairman. He didn't stay for lunch or a drink, but called his chauffeur and returned to London. It was 9 June 1969.

Carr bitterly recalled that it was on 24 October 1968 Murdoch had written to him: 'I will certainly hope for, and support, the continuance of a member of the Carr family as chairman, and I hope you will continue in this capacity.' It had taken him a little over seven months to gain full control.

Carr had to decide. Should he go quickly? These were his words to me: 'I had known our paper for many years as a happy place. It could not be happy if Murdoch and I did not agree. I decided to go.'

So in the end it boiled down to a matter of terms, as it usually does. Carr became life-president and consultant to the end of his contract. He was still a rich man but now without power or influence.

At a board meeting on 19 June 1969 there was one item of business: Carr's resignation from the chair and appointment as president. Not one word of regret was expressed, not one reference to his services over many years. The proceedings took less than five minutes.

Then the directors filed into a large room at the Charing Cross Hotel for the annual meeting, and once more took their places. When Carr announced his decision to go there were murmurs of sympathy from shareholders, who didn't have a clue about the tough dealing behind the scenes. Some of the women present were in tears.

Afterwards, the board met formally to elect Murdoch Chairman. The resolution was moved by Clive Carr, who said that Murdoch had the full support of the Carr family. This was received in silence. Mark Chapman-Walker seconded the resolution and the vote was taken. I didn't put my hand up. Murdoch took the chair with the following words in his abrasive Australian voice: 'Thank you, gentlemen, I don't think there is any other business.'

Looking at the correspondence, some years later, I am still fascinated by the speed with which Murdoch worked.

In January 1969 he told Carr how much better he was looking and, at the same time, explained that he was buying about a million of Jackson's shares, which would not affect their arrangement.

In March he wrote again about Carr's improved health, but complained that Carr was speaking to senior executives. He would, however, continue to respect Carr's position as Chairman. At the same time he asked for Carr's resignation from all subsidiary companies.

In June Murdoch asked for Carr's resignation from the chairmanship because he was worried about Carr's health, which had prevented him from carrying out his duties. He hoped Carr would go quietly; if he didn't, he would have to be voted out, adding that he, Murdoch, now had virtual control. There was, of course, a financial pay-off and Carr could be president. That was a sinecure.

And so an era ended. There was no farewell dinner party, no presentation. I asked Murdoch if it should be mentioned in the paper that Sir William had been made life-president. The answer was: 'The readers don't bloody care.' I did.

At 30 Bouverie Street, Carr's large room, where his father had sat for fifty years, was demolished; his desk was sold, the pictures removed from the walls. In a short time there was a meeting of the new board and, as I looked around the table, I wondered just how long it would be before many more changes would be made. There wasn't long to wait.

Meanwhile a helicopter landed on the lawn at Bentley Wood, and the gravely ill and unconscious Sir William Carr, attended by his doctor, was flown to London for an emergency operation. His surgeon was waiting at St Mary's and Sir William was hurried to the operating theatre. It was a recurrence of the aneurism and for days he lay between life and death.

But this remarkable man recovered, yet again. 'I didn't mind whether I lived or died,' he told me. 'I was sick of everything anyway.' But with amazing resilience he pulled through. He lived on for seven years, but was a shadow of himself. We met a few times and talked about the old days, but he was past caring. He sometimes walked in his garden attended by his male nurse, but did little else. He died, a broken man, almost forgotten. No one from the News of the World attended his funeral. I was there.

# 27 Goodbye to All That

I soon discovered that Murdoch and I had different views about the functions of an Editor. When he changed a contents bill I had approved, I told him that the Editor was responsible for the contents of the paper and posters on the streets: 'This is editorial business,' I said. In April 1969 I was unhappy about editorial changes, and I did not like Murdoch's instruction that, when I wanted to send a correspondent abroad, I should speak to him about it. I took not the slightest notice. I was engaged to edit the paper and that's what I intended to do. In a hundred years no Editor of the News of the World, had been given instructions of that kind. Murdoch was mystified. He said to a senior member of the board: 'Is the Editor allowed to do as he likes?' The answer was: 'Yes — in editorial matters.'

I recalled how, many years earlier, Sir Emsley Carr had got out of the Editor's chair when Lord Riddell tried to give him an instruction saying: 'Either you edit the paper or I do.' That was our tradition.

Murdoch was used to telling Editors what to do, and I was used to having my own way. That, in a nutshell, was the difficulty. A clash was inevitable. To the Royal Commission on the Press, Carr had said: 'I cannot remember issuing a directive to the Editor. The policy of this paper is laid down by the board and the Editor interprets it.' I was resolved not to change the situation, for I believed it to be right, no matter who was chief shareholder and Chairman.

Murdoch's way was different. 'I did not come all this way not to interfere,' he said. He might have talked about co-operation or working together, but not 'interfering'. Those who knew us both said there was a clash of temperament. I thought there was a clash of principles.

On 3 May I left for a holiday in Spain and was lying in the sun in Marbella when I was called to the telephone. It was my personal assistant in London who thought I should know that Murdoch was making big changes in the lay-out of the paper. The leader page had disappeared. I left my long-suffering wife sunbathing and took the next plane home. As I left, my wife said that she would go to a bullfight. I felt I might be going to something similar.

I hurried to the airport and sat thinking about this new development. Murdoch was removing the leader page in my absence and without consultation. I could not believe it; the leader page was a most vital part of the paper. In it were the serious views of the key writers of the day; this was the page that was quoted the world over and without which the paper would be completely out of balance. Not only was I angry that it should have been done without reference to me, but I thought it a serious mistake. We had to have balance; news, sport, serious well-written opinion, investigative reporting, court reports — each was as important as the other. To drop the leader page confirmed me in my view that Murdoch didn't understand what the paper was all about.

I arrived at the office after the first edition had gone to Press and went to see Murdoch. I told him of my concern. 'The leader page must go back in the next edition.' To my astonishment it did. On reflection, I wondered exactly what I would have done had it not done so. I think I should have gone to the composing room and asked the printer to make up a leader page, and then we would have seen whether it would have been put on the machines.

Murdoch, by the way, told Carr he didn't agree with my version of this scene. 'I know what Stafford is after,' he said (meaning a golden handshake) 'and he won't get it from me.' How wrong! All I wanted to do was edit the paper. It was in my mind that, many years earlier when Marlow was Editor of the Mail, Northcliffe had interfered in the composing room. 'Get out,' said Marlow. 'It's your privilege to sack me in the morning, but I'm the boss now.' Northcliffe left the composing room and Marlow stayed.

I wrote a memorandum explaining my views:

As Editor, I am responsible for the newspaper and its contents. The responsibility is both traditional and inveterate. Whether present or absent, or whether, indeed, he has actual knowledge of all the particular contents of the paper, his responsibility remains. This is true in law — e.g., on an application to the High Court for alleged contempt or on a claim for libel — or in ethics or morality — on a complaint to the Press Council — or generally, in accordance with the long-established custom of Fleet Street. The Editor is the servant of the board, and contractually answerable to the board and the managing director. But this does not mean that the chief executive, acting independently of the board, can take his chair, seek to discharge his functions or introduce fundamental editorial changes in the paper, without consultation.

I handed the memorandum to the company secretary and returned to Spain on 20 May. At 8.30 the following evening, while dressing for dinner, I received the following cable: 'Hereby instruct you return England immediately for conference Thursday morning. Murdoch.'

'Well,' I said to my wife. 'that is the first time an Editor of the News of the World has had that sort of order. What shall I do? Ignore it and finish our holiday?' 'Certainly not,' she said, 'go back and have it out. The bloody holiday is spoilt anyway.' She began to pack and I ordered a bottle of champagne, thinking, let battle commence. But there was an interruption. A telephone call from London and a voice saying: 'Murdoch here, forget all cables, don't come back, we will meet on 5 June. We will do nothing until my return from Australia, and I have had a chance to talk to you.' I told Dibbie what was said. 'Unpack,' I said. 'To hell with that,' she cried, 'I'm not going to unpack and pack again. We're for off.'

On 1 June I met Murdoch by chance. He had come to live near me and he invited me to his house. 'The time has come for me to exert my full authority,' he said. 'I propose that you become editorial director, same arrangements as now, same period of contract, car, driver and secretary, but subject to two conditions. I will not ask you to leave the organisation board immediately, but probably in six months, when I may reconstruct it. There may be fewer members. You can remain on the newspaper board.' I told him I would think it over.

To put my views straight I drafted a letter to Murdoch setting out the position as I saw it, reminding him that although he might now be chief proprietor, he was not the sole proprietor, and the board was answerable to all shareholders, and I had been appointed to it at a meeting of all shareholders. I did not feel it right to resign from the top board as he suggested.

Three sayings kept coming into my head. The first by James Maxton: 'If you can't ride two horses at the same time you shouldn't be in the bloody circus.' The second, Truman's maxim: 'If you can't stand the heat of the stove then get out of the kitchen.' And third, Winston's quip: 'It does not necessarily add to your dignity to stand on it.' However, nothing happened for several months and I carried on as usual. Murdoch went off on one of his usual trips to Australia, but before going he gave a lunch at the Ritz and asked me to sit at his left. 'Thank you, Stafford, for all you have done,' he said. 'Now what?' I thought. Another two months passed before I found out.

There was a note on my desk when I arrived at my office on 26 February 1970. It was from my personal assistant, Joan, and it read laconically: 'Mr Murdoch would like to see you at 12 o'clock.' Was it my dismissal? I had thought of it several times before and had twice put my private papers in a couple of suitcases and taken them to my flat. Twice I had brought them back. Now I just kept the suitcases handy.

What had I done this time? True, we had sharp words the previous evening at the conference. He didn't think much of the last issue. I had liked it, and said so. But to me this was only a vigorous exchange of opinion, which, in all my years on the paper, I had never failed to express. I believed an Editor should edit; that was his job. I put it this way: newspaper proprietors, acting for the board, should appoint an Editor, give him his brief, tell him to get on with it, and support him through thick and thin until he was fired.

Murdoch didn't see it that way. He wanted to read proofs, write a leader if he felt like it, change the paper about and give instructions to the staff. I wouldn't allow that. He once appointed a man to the editorial staff without my knowledge. Naturally I ignored the newcomer, which was unfair to him. But there was a principle at stake. Editors should appoint their own staff, and there couldn't be two Editors.

I also reflected that I was out on a limb. Carr, my old friend, was no longer in the chair. Chapman-Walker had taken another job, and some other old colleagues had disappeared. Murdoch controlled the board and the votes. Hislop, the racing correspondent, a sportsman and great character, owner of the wonderful horse Brigadier Gerard, had 'given him a raspberry'. He called Murdoch 'a man with a lot of money and few manners'. Murdoch wrote: 'Thank you for your offensive letter. You are sacked; send your car back.' Hislop retorted: 'I've already resigned, come and get the car.' Two celebrated correspondents, Henry Cotton a top man in golf, and Douglas Bader, the flying ace and national hero, had also gone. What a shambles! Oh dear! That was not the way we used to do things. And there was my friend, Len Slingsby, the advertisement director, first to be fired. He went to court to get his money.

These were my thoughts as I waited for my appointment.

I was ushered in. 'I want your resignation,' said Murdoch. 'I never resign,' I said. He suggested I should see a solicitor. 'Don't worry,' I rejoined, 'I've seen a solicitor.' I walked out of his room. The whole episode had taken three minutes. No reason was given for my dismissal, and no mention ever made of my services over twenty-five years as reporter, sub-editor, Editor and director. When you cut a man's throat maybe it's best to do it quickly and not saw through. Someone had said that when Murdoch fired Editors he cried. This time, I thought, he'll cry because of the money he'll have to pay me and I'll cry because it isn't enough. The three-minute interview inspired an old friend, another sacked Editor, to wire: 'Why did it take three minutes, you talkative bastard?'

That night the London evenings made the story their splash. The Evening Standard said it was a £100,000 pay-off; a slight exaggeration, I may say. They described me as benign and jovial, which was rather nice, that the circulation was up 389,000 over the previous six months, and it was still the largest in the world — a million over its nearest rival. I liked that too.

It was a hectic day. No longer was I interviewing people, I was being interviewed. Anthony Parkinson wrote in the Evening Standard:

Stafford Somerfield, the 59-year-old £17,500-a-year Editor of the News of the World for the last 10 years, was fired today by his chairman, Australian Rupert Murdoch, 39, in a three-minute noon interview.

Cigar-smoking, Mr Somerfield stood in the bar at the Falstaff in Fleet Street surrounded by colleagues and friends this afternoon and said: 'I had a message at 10.30 this morning that Mr Murdoch wanted to see me at noon. I thought it was about a new feature. Then he asked for my resignation. No reason was given.'

This afternoon when Mr Murdoch arrived at the News of the World offices he had 'nothing to say'. Asked if he would be making a statement later, he said: 'I doubt it.'

Mr Somerfield had a seven-year contract with the News of the World and will get a £100,000 golden handshake plus a 'top hat' pension.

Back in the Falstaff Mr Somerfield talked of his years with the paper which he joined in 1945, after leaving the Gloucesters in which he served as a major. He held the posts of Assistant Editor, Northern Editor and Deputy Editor before taking over the editorship.

'I have very much enjoyed working for a quarter of a century with the News of the World, and have been very proud to have been for 10 years Editor of the Sunday paper with the largest circulation,' he said.

As colleagues discussed the loss of the benign, jovial editor, Mr Somerfield said: 'Perhaps I have been too nice.' He mentioned the circulation figures of the News of the World. Audit Bureau of Circulation statistics show an increase of 389,000 over the last six months, and the gap between the News of the World and the People — its nearest rival — is now more than 1,000,000.

Said Tiny Lear, Mr Somerfield's deputy: 'He's a marvellous chap … never any recriminations, never any inquests, and always the thought "let's get on with the next job".' Tiny Lear joined the Army with Mr Somerfield.

Mr Somerfield's secretary, Joan Batt, said: 'He likes to say I've been with him for a quarter of a century, but it's really only 24 years'. Miss Batt added that when he became Editor the staff was divided. He pulled them together, formed a new team and had the boys behind him'.

Wasn't that kind of her? Bless her heart. She died suddenly not such a long time after.

After that came radio and television interviews and a session in El Vinos with old friends. Three other Editors joined in, but none of my colleagues of the board, they were busy elsewhere. One of Murdoch's men always seemed to be there. Where I spent that night I shall never know. That had happened to me once before in Fleet Street back in 1939. I woke up in a strange bedroom. In the other twin bed was a mysterious figure. Who was it? I uncovered the face. Sleeping peacefully was the night editor of the News Chronicle. We had drowned our sorrows as Hitler marched into Poland and I knew the war was about to begin. Then I had dressed, gone home, changed into uniform and didn't return to Fleet Street for six years.

And now Murdoch had sacked me. This thought saddened me: rich men, uncaring, had fought for money and power; in the end Professor Jackson had a couple of millions more; Maxwell had to foot the bill for his abortive effort; Carr was ousted and stricken; Murdoch was triumphant. But what about the others like Chapman-Walker, the managing director, who never recovered; Slingsby, the advertisement director, who was sacked; star editorial men had gone; not to mention the Editor. Bill Hardcastle, one time Editor of the Mail and television personality said I laughed all the way to the bank. I wept when no one was looking.

# 28 My Way

My staff gave me a dinner in the cellars of the Cheshire Cheese in Fleet Street, and, surrounded by wine bottles, I said it was in a Fleet Street pub I got my job, so it was appropriate that I should say farewell in one. I was appointed in five minutes and sacked in three.

The father of the editorial chapel said: 'Perhaps our few disagreements can be put down to the turbulent times. Certainly working with you to produce the paper has never been dull, and often exciting. In the history of this great newspaper, today marks the end of an era.'

No member of the management attended; there was no gift of a gold watch from them and not one line in my own paper although all the others played it big. One said the 'news was world-shaking', but even I admit that that was going a bit far. We all laughed at a telegram that said: 'Suggest black velvet [Guinness and champagne] for sad bereavement,' and at the true story of a Fleet Street executive who took me to dinner and gave great hopes of a new job, only to dash them by saying to me over brandy and cigars: 'How exactly do you get a seven-year contract?' I was sitting with one in my pocket.

I recalled Editors of the past, particularly the one who insisted on a complimentary dinner before he undertook the job in case he didn't get one after. He didn't. I recalled that, three years earlier, I had proposed at a board meeting that an appropriate gift might mark my distinguished services. Well, no one else did. I got a gold pencil, suitably inscribed. Then, bless them, the editorial staff who attended in force, presented me with a tape-recorder — a gift of my own choice.

I advised my colleagues that it was wise to recognise when the moment for going was good. When I went on a world tour, a year earlier, my cabin overflowed with exotic flowers. Now, when I left for ever there wasn't even a daisy. My greatest thrill, I said, had been the take-over battle, the battle of 'Maxwell House', and to those who said that we were over the hill, I quoted the latest circulation figures of six and a half million selling at 8d., a million ahead of our nearest rival. It couldn't be bad.

I reminded them of the words of the wise Lord Goodman: 'Efficiency is only one factor in the scheme of human affairs, and human happiness rates higher than human competence.' I saw no reason why 'efficiency and happiness' should not go together.

The paper had been my mistress, and I objected when a strange man took her away from me. I loved her. That was something Murdoch never understood; he thought I manoeuvred my departure so that I could grab some money. I like money, but newspapers more. No one had expressed the pain of leaving better than Anthony Eden, later Lord Avon, the Foreign Secretary. When he decided he could no longer continue to war with Prime Minister, Neville Chamberlain, he wrote: 'I had enjoyed every moment of the work; it was the breath of life to me. Not only would I now rarely see friends with whom I had worked daily for so long, but I had also a conceit, which I hope was pardonable, that I could do the job if only I could have my way.' That was it exactly.

After many drinks I said goodbye to Fleet Street, declaring 'Let there be no moaning at the bar,' and went out with the words of Frank Sinatra's song:

> The record shows,
> I took the blows,
> And did it my way.

Next day I signed on at the Labour Exchange, but they

wouldn't give me a penny of unemployment pay, though I'd paid in for forty years. They said I didn't qualify, but why? Everyone else seemed to, and it was months before my 'handshake' was agreed. But I got some fun out of it, taking the matter up to Dick Crossman, and when he left office he sent the correspondence to the Conservative Minister, Sir Keith Joseph, with some relief I imagine. Sir Keith wouldn't play ball. Anyway, it was a good try and yielded a good story.

In retrospect, it is easy to say that the battle for the News of the World should never have happened, but it's true. If Sir William Carr, our Chairman, had been a fit man I don't think he would have taken Rupert Murdoch as an ally. We could have won without him, but our knight was wounded and bleeding. It was the ally from within who won.

Murdoch showed boldness, shrewd judgement, courage and opportunism in flying to London to seize a heaven-sent opportunity to get into Fleet Street. It was a brilliant stroke to come in on the winning side and a tough one to turn on Carr who helped him. Today his interests also lie in New York and Australia, and he is a big figure in Fleet Street where he owns a News of the World that continues to thrive and a bustling, successful young Sun.

That evening I faced the television cameras once again. All I remember was one interviewer saying: 'Thank you Mr Murdoch,' to which I replied, 'I'm not Murdoch; I'm the one who got fired.' And to another who asked: 'What are you going to do now?' the answer had to be 'Have a drink'. Next morning I cleared out my desk and went to see Murdoch.

I gave him my keys, told him that all was in order and that I was going round saying goodbye. 'That's quick,' he said. 'It's very civilised of you.' I replied: 'We were civilised at 30, Bouverie Street.'

As a newspaperman I was interested to see how the papers rated the story. The evenings splashed it and it was a page one top in the mornings, including The Times.

197

Murdoch's Sun gave it a paragraph, tucked away. Overseas they gave it a good show.

The Observer made the best comment on our take-over battle.

> It was not just the old story of a cosy family company closing its ranks against the ruthless intruder. Here were two intruders, well-matched and oddly similar — two hulking men, both looking like pugilists with chests out and arms swinging, involving more and more bankers and shareholders in their fight. Not surprisingly, perhaps, the carnage was enormous; the victory may well have been Pyrrhic, and looking into the story, it is hard to see how anyone has won.

I could have told them who had lost.

As ever, it was Lord Goodman who put the whole business of take-overs into perspective. Writing in the Sunday Times on 12 January 1969, he said:

> The servants of a company are often more numerous than its shareholders. Their stake in the company is demonstrably more important to them than is the investment to the shareholders. But their employer can be changed without reference to them, without their approval, and without regard to the consequences upon them, including loss of employment. If the paramount objective were one of efficiency and of economy, there might indeed be arguments that a change of this sort should be permitted, but there is no evidence that, in most cases, efficiency, or economy, are factors that are germane to the transfer of ownership, which is unashamably inspired by profit motivations. If, as admittedly happens, greater efficiency and economy do result, this is not a certain, but a chance and incidental result.
>
> That one man should have his job and security

imperilled, to make another man richer, is a distasteful notion in a modern society, without taking into account the public interest. The decision is arrived at without consultation with customers, suppliers, persons engaged in allied or service trades, or without a myriad other interests, which may add up in financial and emotional content to a great deal more than the value of the shareholding.

# 29 Every Day a Sunday

When one door closes another opens, or so they say. I left the 'rat race' and returned to the countryside I love, and amused myself writing a couple of books and a column about pedigree dogs, which the ever-watchful Guardian had to christen 'Woolfs of the World'. I put down my thoughts for the Sunday Times.

Retirement is not so gloomy. I decided, while walking across the fields with my dog. Let me tell about my experience. It was a good morning for thinking about it: a fresh wind, warm rain, the golden leaves being blown about, and my beautiful Doberman bitch in her gleaming black satin coat, running and leaping with joy. I was content.

Life is very different from the days when I edited a newspaper that millions read every Sunday. Those were hard exciting times, but now I realise that, apart from taking part in the war, I have thought of nothing other than newspapers for more than forty years. There are other things. Friends, I have a few, say: But what do you do with yourself? I come up with the reply: 'I don't know how I found time to work', and there's a lot of truth in it. Of course the experts will say I'm still in the honeymoon period, but its getting on for nine months now and something pregnant could have been expected. But there's no sign: I really love my freedom and a less-demanding job that gives me time to sit and look. It is very satisfying.

There are changes. I no longer live in a London flat, lunch regularly at the Savoy Grill, go to first nights, talk endlessly in Fleet Street pubs and work like a beaver. Do I miss these things? Certainly I miss writing leaders putting the nation straight! I miss directing a lively temperamental staff. I miss invitations to No. 10, to Buckingham Palace and everywhere else. Nobody hoped I would be at the party conferences this year, thank God, and there won't be Christmas cards from Ted and Harold.

But there are other things. Two sharp lessons in my life taught me something. When the fingers were blown off my right hand (by a grenade) I learnt to write with the stumps. I was once a theatre-critic. Managers welcomed me with smiles, drinks and good seats. I was young enough then to have thought they cared about me. That would have been very silly. When I was fired from this job no one wanted to know. Someone else would get the smiles, the drinks, and the good seats. But I got the lessons free. If you lose your right hand, there's always the left. And, in my case, after the theatre there was another job. Now I spend more time in the country. I'm organising clearance of a pond choked by bullrushes; Moses, doing the job, is twirling round in a flat-bottomed boat as though in a dodgem car. I am planning to reinforce the banks and plant primroses. We have laid a lawn, built a wall and cleared the rubbish. If this is the honeymoon, I'm liking it.

The Sunday Times headlined the article 'Every day a Sunday'. Why? Because that's the day Sunday-paper men sleep.

# Exit

I wrote 'end of story' here. But it wasn't the end. For seven years, during the period of my consultancy with Murdoch's newspapers, I was barred from working for others in the same field — that was part of the pay-off. But with that behind me, my book was accepted and I couldn't resist an offer to write a column for a country newspaper. That is where I came in fifty years ago, and the game still has the same thrill for me. It's true what they say about the smell of printers' ink.

When the seven years was up, I thought it would be amusing to look in again at 30 Bouverie Street and 'hand in my cards'. Murdoch was in another part of the world, but Alick McKay (afterwards Sir Alick) his 'stand-in', was there. He'd had ghastly trouble. His wife Muriel was murdered and her body never found. One of the killers telephoned me and asked for a million pounds ransom ... but that's yet another story.

Alick was a courageous man and we had always got on well together. He thought it appropriate that we should 'crack a bottle' on this, my farewell appearance. We drank champagne, joked about the old days, said goodbye, and I walked down the front steps thinking well, that's life. Did I love or hate Fleet Street? I shall never know.